The Long-Term Care Planning Guide

Practical Steps for Making Difficult Choices

BY DON KORN

FOREWORD BY

MICHAEL HALLORAN, CFP, CLTC

HALLORAN FINANCIAL SERVICES

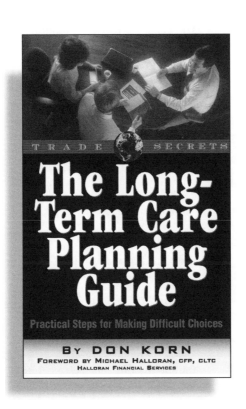

TRADE SECRETS

The Long-Term Care Planning Guide

Practical Steps for Making Difficult Choices

BY DON KORN

FOREWORD BY MICHAEL HALLORAN, CFP, CLTC
HALLORAN FINANCIAL SERVICES

Titles in the Trade Secrets Series

*"Proverbially, death and taxes are life's
only two certainties. A need for long-term care
might not be quite as inescapable,
but it's not far behind."*

— Don Korn

ISBN 1-931611-96-3

Printed in the United States of America.

Contents

Chapter 8

Chapter 9

Chapter 10

The Long-Term Care Planning Guide

Practical Steps for
Making Difficult Choices

Introduction

A fter 22 months in a nursing home, my father died in 1996. My mother and I were with him at the end. They had been happily married for 50 years. Following a severe stroke in 1991, she cared for him at home, which worked well for quite a while. However, his situation, which had been stable for about 18 months, began to deteriorate when he started to have mini-strokes (TIA's). With each TIA, his care became progressively more difficult. Finally, my mother reluctantly agreed that she was putting her health and his physical well being at risk by insisting on keeping him at home. Since his death my mother has referred to my dad's incapacity as her "long goodbye." Many, many widows and widowers have had similar experiences. I am an independent Certified Financial Planner in Boston, Massachusetts. Since 1992, I have discussed long-term care needs with all my financial-planning clients. For those in their 30s and 40s, we talk about what they need to take care of their parents and for those 50 and above, we talk about their own long-term care needs.

Counseling clients on long-term care issues goes beyond your normal financial advice into the realm of lifetime planning. *The Long-Term Care Planning Guide* gives you the information you need to educate yourself, and then your clients, about this critical area. Your clients may believe that government-sponsored Medicare and Medicaid programs will provide their elder health care. They may be opting to self insure and then use Medicaid, unaware that it has the world's largest deductible — basically their entire net worth. Clients need to understand how little money will be left for their healthy spouse if they become disabled. The likelihood of needing long-term care is going up, not down. Medical advances have turned many acute illnesses, which used to kill people, into chronic conditions requiring care. Willard Scott no longer offers birthday greetings to seniors turning 100, because there are too many of them.

With added longevity comes an increasing need for additional elder care. This is a new problem. In 1994, Eldon Weisheit wrote, "Nowadays, the majority of middle-aged people have more parents than they have children." Two-thirds of all the people who ever lived to age 65 are alive today. Your clients need to plan for their elder health care. They need and welcome your help. This care costs so much that neither your client nor the government can afford it. Twenty-five percent of the massive Medicaid budget pays nursing home bills. In Massachusetts, 74% of all patients in nursing homes are funded by Medicaid. To encourage citizens to provide for their own care, the federal government made long-term care insurance premiums tax deductible and long-term care insurance benefit payments income-tax free in 1997. This is a sure sign that the government wants its citizens to care for themselves.

Don Korn's book will make you knowledgeable about aging, government health programs, Medicaid eligibility, Medigap insurance, long-term care insurance and the other items which have made you avoid long-term care planning in your practice. In many situations the planning solution is affordable long-term care insurance. This is a wonderful product which provides care at home as well as in the nursing home. It allows your clients to maintain their independence and provides them with the best health-care choices. My clients, who have been most receptive to long-term care insurance, have been widows. They are realistic and understand that they most likely will not die over a weekend. Dying takes a long time and requires a lot of care. They know this because they cared for their husbands. They hope that their children will be there for them, but they want to be proactive and make preparations themselves. They do not want to be a burden. They want to maintain their independence and provide themselves with the best care possible. They need your help. Make yourself knowledgeable and comfortable with long-term care planning by reading Don's book.

Michael F. Halloran, CFP, CLTC
Halloran Financial Services
Needham, MA

Chapter 1

PLANNING FOR LONG-TERM CARE

A mong your client base, virtually everyone will have long-term care (LTC) concerns, now or in the future, and for a variety of different reasons.

• **Retirees**. The days when people would retire at 65, and die at 75, are long gone. The average life expectancy is well over 80 now, for retirees, and medical advances are taking it still higher. Even the healthiest retiree will one day need care, to some extent, and have to figure out how to pay for it.

• **Pre-retirees**. Younger clients, in their 40s or 50s, worry about their aging parents. Finances are certainly an issue, but so is a need for help in determining the best way to see that care is provided. And, an accident or illness can strike at any age, requiring long-term care for you, your spouse, or your child. Every family needs to plan for such an eventuality, to avoid financial burdens that can result in the loss of a home or other assets.

Long-term care also differs from traditional medical care and can encompass a number of different postures. Long-term care may include help with everyday activities, such as dressing and eating, or it may refer to home health care, nursing home care, adult day care or care in an assisted living facility. And, while most people think of long-term care as something needed only by elderly people, an unforeseen illness or catastrophic accident will make it essential for any person, and every family, to plan for.

Learning about these issues will help you attract and retain clients. On the other hand, if you draw a blank you stand to lose influence to lawyers, doctors, social workers—and to other planners who are up to speed on LTC.

Crisis—and Opportunity

Proverbially, death and taxes are life's only two certainties. A need for long-term care might not be quite as inescapable, but it's not far behind.

Medical advances are not only saving lives, they're extending lives. "Three-score-and-ten" is giving way to four-score-ten, and then some. Some experts see today's 50-year-olds routinely celebrating triple-digit birthdays.

The older people get, the more likely they'll lose their physical or mental abilities—or both. Many "senior seniors" are likely to become incapacitated, in need of constant care.

When the near-inevitable occurs, who will be there to provide that care? An aging spouse? A son or (more often) a daughter, who may have other responsibilities and who may live a continent's width away? The days when an extended family could be counted on to assume responsibility for care of the elderly are long gone.

Increasingly, caregivers will have to be hired to provide long-term care (LTC). Whether this care takes place at home or in an institution, it will be expensive. The longer such care is needed, the greater the drain on a client's budget. Therefore, financial planning certainly should include this possible need.

Family Finances at Risk

Unfortunately, there are no easy answers to this problem. Aging is increasingly a fact of life, the elderly are likely to need custodial LTC, and the costs of such care are bound to increase.

Younger clients, while naturally concerned for the comfort of their elderly relative, can't help but mourn the loss of funds that might be needed for their own retirement or for the education of youngsters.

Over time, serious family issues may be raised as money keeps pouring out.

Nevertheless, there are ways to plan for this problem; indeed, you can provide valuable services for your clients by doing so. That's the purpose of this book—to explain what financial planners realistically can do to help clients cope with the demands of LTC.

Future Shock

When Jim Adams retired, he and his wife Carol felt secure about their future. They had an investment portfolio of $500,000, enough so they were comfortable, if not wealthy. They invested in a healthy mix of stocks and bonds, planning to withdraw a moderate 6%, or $30,000 per year.

Their combined Social Security and pension benefits came to $30,000 per year, for an overall retirement income of $60,000. This would be enough, they assumed, to allow them to enjoy a long and rewarding retirement.

That might have been the case, but Jim was stricken by Alzheimer's disease. At age 73, he entered a nursing home—in an area where nursing homes cost $75,000 per year. Carol, then 68, continued to live independently, at a cost of $35,000 per year.

With $110,000 worth of expenses and $60,000 in income, their savings were swiftly depleted. What's more, as they drew down savings their investment income fell, increasing the amount they had to withdraw from their savings. In six years, their $500,000 nest egg had been reduced to $85,000 and Jim was eligible for Medicaid, a poverty program.

From that point on, Jim's nursing home expenses were covered. In essence, his pension and Social Security checks were sent to the nursing home while Medicaid paid the balance.

Now, however, Carol is only 74, with a 15-year life expectancy. To get her through the rest of her life, she has only $85,000 in investments and a modest benefit from Social Security. She may be forced to sell their house to raise money—and that may create problems with Jim's Medicaid eligibility. Thus, Jim's incapacity has jeopardized Carol's future.

Aging Population

As a financial planner, you are likely to encounter such situations among your clients. At the beginning of the 20th century the average American's life expectancy was under 50 years; by the end of the century that life expectancy was over 75 years. Today, every man who makes it to the "normal" retirement age of 65 can expect to live until 84, while a 65-year-old woman can expect to reach 87.

What's more, those are the averages. Some will die earlier but some will live even longer, to 90 and 95 and 100. Already, there are well over one million Americans over 90 years old, and that demographic group is increasing rapidly.

> **"Without proper planning, long-term care can deplete clients' wealth; but savvy planning can reduce this serious risk to their wealth and welfare."**

Increasing age means increasing reliance on others. Nearly 40% of the men and more than 50% of the women over age 85 need assistance with walking, bathing or eating. That means a tremendous demand for at-home care.

Many of those people, moreover, will wind up needing so much care that institutionalization is the only practical alternative. About 25% of all Americans over age 85 suffer from Alzheimer's disease while another 25% have some other form of dementia. Other elderly Americans have chronic diseases such as Parkinson's, multiple sclerosis, severe arthritis, or stroke that can lead to a need for constant care. Such diseases are progressive and may eventually force those afflicted to stay in an institution.

Of the men who reach age 65, 14%—one out of every seven—will spend at least one year in a nursing home. For women, the proportion is close to one out of three.

Those numbers, remember, apply to one-year stays. Some will need extended stays: 4% of elderly men and 13% of elderly women will spend five years or more in a nursing home.

Are these numbers starting to run together? Keep these highlights in mind:

- Already, there are 35 million people over age 65 in the U.S. The Census Bureau projects this number will reach 80 million by 2050.

- Altogether, three out of five people age 65 or older may need some LTC.

- Two out of five elderly people are likely to spend time in an institution rather than get care at home.

- According to a study published in 2000 in the *Journal of Financial Service Professionals*, 15.2% of people 85 and older live in a nursing home, compared with 1.3% of those in the 65-74 age bracket.

- The same study found that 31.9% of people 85 and older need home health care, compared with 10% of those aged 65-74.

- A married couple can reasonably expect to be retired for more than 20 years.

- Assuming that a married couple both reach age 65, there's a 67% chance that at least one spouse will spend time in a nursing home.

- There's a 10% chance that one spouse will be in a nursing home for more than five years.

- Those most likely to wind up in a nursing home are widows who are over 85.

Loosening Family Ties

Ideally, the elderly will be cared for by a loved one, at home, but that's not always possible. When an 84-year-old man can't walk and can't remember names, it's not likely that his 81-year-old wife will be able to care for him. As for their 52-year-old daughter, she may live 100 miles away, trying to get her career back on track while she and her husband are wrestling with college bills incurred by their children.

Thus, it's not likely that your clients can count on relatives to care for them at home. They'll probably have to hire someone, and that can be expensive. In 2000, the American Council of Life Insurers reported that:

- The average cost of a nursing home is projected at $190,600 per year in 2030 (when today's 50-year-olds are nearing 80), up from $44,100 in 2000.

- Assisted living, which currently averages $25,300 per year, could cost $109,300 in 2030.

- The cost of home health care is forecast to rise from $61 to $260 per visit, or $68,000 per year, at five visits per week, between now and 2030.

- If clients need full-time, live-in help the cost will be much greater. Nationwide, daily home-care costs average $36,000 per year.

For many elderly people, home care will not be adequate, even with live-in caregivers, so they'll be moved to a nursing home — at considerable expense. The average cost of staying in a nursing home might be $44,100, but in some areas, nursing homes cost $90,000 or more per year.

That is, a five-year stay at an "average" nursing home will cost more than $220,000. If your clients are "fortunate" enough to live in a high-cost area of the U.S., that stay might cost more than half-a-million dollars!

Supply-Side Shortfall

Now, you might think that the supply would adjust to reflect increasing demand. As more elderly need long-term care, more nursing homes will be built to accommodate them.

You might think so, but that's by no means the case. To state governments, nursing homes are expensive because the states bear some of the costs involved in paying for destitute residents. Therefore, several states restrict the construction of new nursing homes.

When expanding demand meets stagnant supply something has to give, and that something is price restraint. In the past few years the average nursing home cost has increased by 50%, and further increases are certain.

Clients who are in their 60s now can certainly expect to pay $60,000, $80,000 or more for a year in a nursing home.

Medicare Won't Help

How do clients expect to pay these bills? Perhaps they believe that Medicare will pick up the tab. After all, Medicare is federal "health insurance" for the elderly.

In truth, Medicare won't pay for "custodial care," which is what most people need in a nursing home. Residents receive custodial care when someone helps them with bathing, dressing, eating, etc.

What will Medicare pay for? Circumstances vary, but the bottom line is, not much. Medicare pays some of the cost for strictly defined medical care, at home or in a skilled nursing home. However, Medicare won't pay for extended long-term care, the kind most likely to put a strain on your finances and your family's equilibrium.

Thus, Medicare paid for less than 12% of the nation's nursing-home bills, as of 1998, the most recent period for which data are available. Instead, the largest amount (over 46%) of money paid to nursing homes came from Medicaid, a federal-state poverty program, followed by out-of-pocket payments from residents and their families.

> "Qualifying for Medicaid provides scant consolation because the nursing-home resident is virtually destitute."

In the "real world," as the saying goes, many people who are in nursing homes begin by paying their own way, $3,000 or $4,000 or $5,000 per month. If they stay in the home for any length of time, their savings will be completely wiped out. Then they're "poor," officially and actually, so Medicaid will step in and maintain the payments. Beyond those payments, qualifying for Medicaid provides scant consolation because the nursing-home resident is virtually destitute.

Surely "the government" will "do something" about LTC. After all, aren't the news media constantly running articles about the political power of the elderly?

In truth, the government is unlikely to expand its role in paying for long-term care. Such a burden would be tremendously expensive, out of sync with the small-government, balanced-budget philosophy that reigns today. Some tinkering might be done, such as modest tax credit for caregivers' expenses, but there's no federal program on the horizon that would truly pick up the bills for long-term care.

Many seniors own "Medigap" policies, to cover gaps in Medicare coverage, such as prescription drugs. However, the biggest gap in Medicare (long-term care) is not covered by Medigap insurance, nor by other forms of health insurance, nor by managed care.

When it comes to long-term care, clients have these choices:

- Pay the bills personally.
- Rely upon someone else's generosity to pay the bills.
- Become impoverished so that Medicaid will pay the bills.
- Buy special-purpose insurance to pay some, or all, of the bills.

Indeed, it has been suggested that clients and their relatives may attempt to hold planners liable if they don't suggest the purchase of LTC insurance.

In the chapters that follow, these alternatives will be examined. The bottom line: without proper planning, LTC can deplete clients' wealth; but savvy planning can reduce this serious risk to their wealth and welfare.

Chapter 2

DEFINING THE TERMS
Putting the "Long"
Into Long-Term Care

I f you are going to help clients cope with the demands of LTC, it's vital that you know some of the terminology. As the phrase "long-term care" suggests, some of your clients will reach a stage where they'll need care from a third party. Often, that care will have to go on for many years—that's where the expense can come in.

To begin with, there are two distinctions to keep in mind:

• **Skilled care.** Clients who are ill or injured will need medical care, often from a physician, probably in a hospital. Such care tends to be relatively brief.

Following medical care, skilled nursing care may be needed to provide for a recovery and prevent a relapse. Again, this care probably will be needed for a short time period: weeks or months.

• **Custodial care.** This expression refers to assistance with day-to-day routines, such as bathing, dressing and eating. Often, such routines are called "activities of daily living," or ADLs.

This type of care need not be administered by a physician or a skilled nurse; in many cases, any competent and compassionate individual can provide such care. However, the need for this care can go on for years, so this is truly LTC. In many cases, an extensive need for custodial care can be financially devastating.

Preservation of Independence

Elderly clients (or the elderly parents of middle-aged clients) frequently go through a progression that gradually increases their need for LTC. Many elderly people begin this progression by living independently — that is, they maintain their own home and go about their lives as always.

At some point, though, help is needed. Perhaps someone has to clean their house or prepare their meals; they might need someone to remind them to take their medicine.

At this point, *home health care* might be needed. Some trusted individual or individuals (perhaps provided by an agency), can come into the elderly person's home to provide the needed care. In many cases, home health care aides will have to live in the elderly person's home, to provide the desired level of care. Such extensive care will be expensive, but most people like the idea of receiving care in their own home, rather than in an institution.

Home vs. Nursing Home

Indeed, most older Americans, no matter how frail, dread having to go into a nursing home. Fortunately, only 5% of the elderly reside in institutions. Instead, most seniors stay in their own homes. One prime benefit of such arrangements is that familiarity helps them retain their mental abilities. They keep in contact with neighbors, friends, merchants, and so on. Living amid their own furnishings provides comfort, too.

What About Costs?

As we've indicated, living in a nursing home can be extremely expensive — in some areas of the U.S., annual fees can top $100,000!

However, aging at home can be costly, too, especially if the resident needs extensive services, which might include:
- at-home caregivers, full- or part-time
- home-delivered or home-prepared meals
- housekeeping
- transportation services, including rides to medical appointments

Help Is Available: Recommended Resources

What might you suggest to clients to help them provide care for a loved one without overpaying? You can recommend that they get in touch with:

- **The local Agency on Aging.** Most communities have such an agency, which can help with everything from checking into caregivers to legal assistance. The local phone book should have a listing.

- **Eldercare Locator.** This is a nationwide directory of local resources. Call 800-677-1116 for information.

- **Children of Aging Parents (CAPS).** CAPS (800-227-7294) is a support group that provides counseling.

- **National Association of Professional Geriatric Care Managers**. To order a directory of its members, which lists credentials, call 520-881-8008.

Consider a Care Manager

You might suggest working work with a geriatric care manager (GCM). This is a new profession, comprised mainly of social workers or registered nurses.

Generally, these professionals will visit the older person at home, spend 60 to 90 minutes assessing the situation, and recommend a course of action. Then, the GCM will monitor the person's activities, if desired, and help make suitable arrangements.

Your clients can expect to pay $50 to $150 per hour for a GCM's services. For that, they'll receive general counseling and support as well as:

- **Liaison with other professionals.** A GCM will bring in doctors, lawyers, and financial planners who specialize in geriatric services.

- **Oversight of caregivers.** A GCM can hire people to care for your client at home and monitor progress.

- **Incompetency planning**. When clients reach the point when they no longer can manage their own affairs, a GCM can help the family navigate the maze of conservatorship or guardianship procedures.

If your clients are interested in a GCM, advise them to approach the engagement just as they'd hire any professional:

- Ask about credentials and check references.

- Get a written letter of engagement that spells out the fees.

- Find out if the GCM will be available, in case of emergency, and if there's a backup person to call.

As always, chemistry counts. Your clients should feel this is a person with whom they're comfortable and who is likely to truly care for their loved one.

> "The more involved your clients are in the community, the more likely they'll be able to stay in their own homes."

Staying Active

Other than suggesting that clients retain a GCM, what can you as a financial planner recommend to help clients retain their independence?

You can urge them to remain active. Everyone needs interests, a reason to get up in the morning. The more involved your clients are in the community, the more likely they'll be able to stay in their own homes.

Therefore, you should encourage them to participate in any activity that they'll truly enjoy, from swimming lessons to bridge to an investment club. Do what you can to resolve any problems, such as a lack of transportation.

Nevertheless, the truth is that the elderly spend much of their time at home rather than in the swimming pool or at the bridge club. Thus, you should try to encourage activities for them to do at home, too.

Large-print books, publications, and crossword puzzles can keep the mind strong even as the eyes weaken. TV is an inevitable fact of life for stay-at-homes, so be sure they're signed up for full-service cable TV, with all of the elderly person's favorite shows.

When you deal with elderly clients, look out for early warning signs. Forgetfulness, slovenly appearance, falling, and not taking medicine are all indications of gradual deterioration. The classic example, though, is a tendency to forget paying bills for vital services such as heat, electricity, and the phone.

When you see these signs, ask your client's physician for advice. Often, it may be time to hire a companion or a visiting nurse. Some communities have volunteer companions, meals-on-wheels, senior van routes, and so on. The groups listed previously can help your client's family find them.

Safe at Home

Independent living is appealing to the elderly but there may be perils, too. If you're trying to help an elderly person stay at home, make sure that the house is "senior-proof." You might suggest that someone:

- Replace incandescent lights with fluorescents. Move or shade any lights that glare.
- Install night lights in the bedroom, bathroom, and kitchen areas.
- Get rid of throw rugs or tack them down.
- Make sure important items are on shelves or in drawers that are neither too high nor too low. (This is especially important in the kitchen.)
- Replace old chairs or sofas that are too soft to get up from easily.
- Install grab bars and non-slip mats in tubs and showers. (A grab bar by the toilet also is a good idea.)
- Pay extra attention to stairways by checking handrails and installing non-skid treads.
- Move phone and electric cords so they're not on the floor.
- Get a plumber to keep water temperature below 120 degrees to prevent accidental scalding.
- Get an electrician to install a "ground fault circuit interrupter" in the bathroom to prevent electrical shocks.

Assisted Living

All of these efforts, though, may not permit clients to stay in their own home forever. At some point, clients may need more care. Thus, the *assisted living* phenomenon has arisen.

Assisted living is a privately paid (without government support) alternative for people who need some LTC but do not require constant supervision in a nursing home. Typically, in an assisted-living facility, residents have their own apartments with kitchens, communal eating facilities, and access to social activities. Public areas of these facilities resemble hotels rather than hospitals: some assisted-living facilities have hair salons, libraries, ice-cream parlors, and vintage jukeboxes. Antique wedding dresses, for example, might be placed on display in an effort to stimulate residents' memories.

> **"Assisted-living is designed for relatively healthy residents."**

At these facilities, the frail and elderly can get help with daily routines such as bathing and dressing, but not intensive nursing care. Thus, assisted-living is designed for relatively healthy residents. States may bar assisted-living homes from accepting certain kinds of residents, such as those too weak to propel their own wheelchairs. (However, some assisted-living homes will accept those who need extensive care.)

Costly Care

For such amenities, residents (or their families) can expect to pay heavily. In "low-cost" areas, monthly fees start at $3,000, while most residents pay hundreds of dollars per month for extra services, including medical care. Still more may be spent to hire private-duty aides.

Generally, assisted-living homes are lightly regulated, by each individual state, compared with the federal regulatory barriers facing nursing homes. Perhaps as a result, assisted-living facilities generally have much smaller staffs than nursing homes. A typical nursing home (90 beds) might have two registered nurses and three licensed practical nurses on duty at all times, as well as an on-call medical director.

An assisted-living home, by contrast, might have one registered on duty, part of the day (12 hours or less), and no nurse the rest of the time. Residents have to make their own arrangements for medical care.

Assisted-living homes don't provide much in the way of doctors or nurses because people on staff aren't allowed to give medication to residents. They can coax but they can't put a pill into someone's mouth. (In general, they may give insulin shots.)

By contrast, a key function of nursing homes is administering medication, via pills, injections, or IV.

Adult Day-Care

As mentioned, some assisted-living facilities will accept and retain residents who need extensive care—as long as they're able to pay. Nevertheless, there may come a time when assisted-living facilities will not be adequate.

Then what can be done? One option is to arrange for the elderly person to stay at an *adult day-care center* during the work day, and have family members provide custodial care the rest of the time. With this arrangement, the elderly individual still spends a great deal of time with loved ones.

But not every family has a willing and able middle-aged caregiver with room for an elderly individual. Therefore, some seniors need to be institutionalized, in a *nursing home*. There, residents can expect full-time custodial care and access to whatever medical care might be necessary.

No one wants to wind up in a nursing home, and few people want their elderly relatives there. As a financial planner, you can help suggest viable alternatives; if they don't work, you can help prepare your clients to handle the costs of a long nursing home stay.

Chapter 3

GOVERNMENT RESOURCES
What Clients Can — and Can't — Expect

T wo facts have emerged from the previous chapters. One, clients and their aging parents are likely to need LTC as they grow older; two, LTC may be extremely expensive.

Clients may think that "the government" will help with this issue. In truth, the government offers some programs in this area but clients shouldn't expect too much.

Medicare's Short-Term View

What can clients expect from Medicare, the federal health insurance program for those over age 65? Medicare covers many illnesses but it provides little help when dealing with the need for LTC. Medicare provides some nursing home coverage but not any "long-term" care. Instead, Medicare Part A (hospital insurance) provides up to 100 days of skilled nursing care per benefit period in a "certified skilled nursing facility."

A "certified skilled nursing facility" is a place that offers skilled nursing care or skilled rehabilitation services, plus other medical services. It must be certified under the Medicare Act to have met high standards for care. (It may be a specially qualified long-term care facility, part of a hospital or a rehabilitation center.)

Skilled nursing facilities provide the necessary level of medical and round-the-clock nursing care for the patient who does not require the specialized care of a hospital. To be certified by Medicare, a skilled nursing facility must meet these standards:

- It must be licensed in accordance with state and local laws, including all applicable laws pertaining to staff, licensing and registration, fire, safety, communicable diseases, etc.

- It must have a governing body legally responsible for policies and the appointment of a qualified administrator.

- It must have one or more physicians on call at all times to cover an emergency.

- It must have 24-hour nursing care services.

- It must have a sufficient number of nurses on duty at all times, including at least one registered nurse employed full time.

- It must place a registered nurse or qualified, licensed practical nurse in charge of each tour of duty.

- It also must offer a continuing educational program for all nursing personnel.

In addition, to be certified a facility must comply with Medicare requirements in the areas of resident rights, quality of care, dental care, infection control, relationships with hospitals, drug dispensing, recordkeeping, rehabilitation services, social services, food service, activities, building maintenance, and admission practices.

> Medicare provides some nursing home coverage but not any "long-term" care. Instead, Medicare Part A (hospital insurance) provides up to 100 days of skilled nursing care per benefit period in a "certified skilled nursing facility."

As you can gather, not every facility billing itself as a "nursing home" is going to meet these criteria and become eligible for Medicare coverage. Even when Medicare's requirements are met by a facility, coverage is limited.

Specifically, Medicare will pay for medically necessary inpatient care in a skilled nursing facility after a hospital stay of at least three days, but only for the first 20 days. For the next 80 days, the patient must pay up to $99 per day (in 2001) before Medicare covers anything.

After 100 days, Medicare checks out and the patient becomes responsible.

Home Care: Strings Attached

If Medicare won't pay for much LTC in a nursing home, what about LTC delivered at home? Again, clients can't expect much LTC coverage.

Under certain conditions, Medicare Part A also pays for home health care as well as 80% of the approved cost for wheelchairs, hospital beds, and other durable medical equipment supplied under the home health care benefit. Medicare may pay the approved costs for home-care visits by a visiting nurse, physical therapist or other approved health care worker. Prior hospitalization is not required.

> **Under certain conditions, Medicare Part A also pays for home health care as well as 80% of the approved cost for wheelchairs, hospital beds, and other durable medical equipment supplied under the home health care benefit.**

However, the patient must be confined to the house and a physician must set up the home health care plan. Generally, coverage is limited to visits that occur two to three times per week for less than an hour apiece. The patient is responsible for paying for all other nursing costs as well as drugs, meals delivered to the home and homemaker services.

Bridging the Medigap

Therefore, financial planners advising clients about LTC should know what they can—and can't—expect from Medicare. Generally, seniors become eligible for Medicare when they reach age 65. Participants pay nothing for Part A, which covers hospital bills; they pay $50 per month (in 2001) for Part B, which covers other medical expenses. (At present, Medicare does not cover prescription drugs but that's likely to change soon.)

In the "standard" Medicare program there are deductibles and co-payments; participants also may have to pay for checkups, immunizations, eyeglasses, and hearing aids. Thus, clients' exposure can be considerable. Many Medicare participants, therefore, take one of two paths to reduce this exposure:

- They enroll in a Medicare HMO.
- They buy a Medicare supplement ("Medigap") policy.

Medicare HMO

Some of the advantages to a Medicare HMO include:

- coordinated care
- lower costs
- guaranteed acceptance — no matter what their health
- little or no paperwork required for claims

In general, Medicare HMOs limit members' choices of doctors and hospitals in return for cost savings. If a client has a strong relationship with his or her physician, enrolling in an HMO where that physician is not affiliated may not be appropriate. On the other hand, clients who have been in an HMO before retirement may find it easy to adjust to a Medicare HMO.

Retirees who relocate also may be well-served in a Medicare HMO. Going into a new environment, as far as health care is concerned, an HMO may provide the patient with more coordinated care.

Beyond the question of medical care, there usually are financial benefits to signing up with a Medicare HMO. Many Medicare HMOs charge little or nothing above the monthly Part B premium; office visits may cost only $10 or so. For this, patients get full hospital and medical coverage, often including preventive care. Prescription drugs may be covered too, although some co-payment may be required.

Medicare HMOs offer other advantages in addition to lower costs. Most Medicare HMOs can't turn away applicants, no matter what their health. Moreover, there is little or no paperwork required for claims in Medicare HMOs.

In order to reap the benefits of a Medicare HMO, participants must choose from a list of specified doctors and hospitals. Usually, one general practitioner is named as your "gatekeeper"; only after the gatekeeper has made a referral may you see a specialist. In practice, referrals may be difficult to come by, because the referring doctor's compensation may be reduced, in some HMOs.

Checkups Before Checks

Clients who are interested in a Medicare HMO should check out the specific terms before signing up. Is dental care included? Is there an annual limit on prescription drugs — and, if so, how high? In some Medicare HMOs, patients have to make higher co-payments for name-brand drugs than for generic pharmaceuticals.

Long-distance care may be critical for clients who travel or maintain two households. In most Medicare HMOs, participants can't get care away from their home area. The only exception is emergency care, and some HMOs enforce that rule strictly. On the other hand, some Medicare HMOs in the North are setting up reciprocal agreements with managed care plans in Florida, Arizona, and other states favored by "snowbirds."

Another option for retirees who travel or split residences is the "point-of-service" Medicare HMO, which enables members to go out-side the network if they're willing to pay some of the doctors' bills. Again, these programs are not standardized, so clients need to look hard to see what restrictions apply.

In recent years, federal cutbacks on Medicare spending have squeezed many Medicare HMOs. Some have increased fees, cut ser-vices, or both. Moreover, some HMOs have dropped out of Medicare altogether, forcing hundreds of thousands of seniors to find another (perhaps less convenient) Medicare HMO or pay higher costs to join traditional Medicare.

Therefore, joining a Medicare HMO presents certain risks that are all but impossible to evaluate beforehand.

A new program, "Medicare Choice," is supposed to open up more options for seniors. As of this writing, though, Medicare Choice has yet to provide many alternatives to Medicare HMOs and traditional Medicare.

Medicare Supplement ("Medigap") Policy

The federal government mandated standardized Medigap policies in 1990. Now, only 10 types of policies can be sold, ranging from basic ("A") through comprehensive ("J"). One company's "E," for example, must offer the same benefits as every other company's "E."

The 10 Standard Medigap Plans									
Coverage	A	B	C	D	E	F	G	H	I	J
Core benefits	✓	✓	✓	✓	✓	✓	✓	✓	✓	✓
Skilled nursing care facility			✓	✓	✓	✓	✓	✓	✓	✓
Hospital deductible		✓	✓	✓	✓	✓	✓	✓	✓	✓
Medical deductible			✓		✓					✓
Excess medical charges						100%	80%		100%	100%
Foreign treatment			80%	80%	80%	80%	80%	80%	80%	80%
At-home recovery				✓			✓		✓	✓
Prescription drugs								Basic	Basic	Extended
Preventive screening					✓					✓

Source: *Guide to Health Insurance for People With Medicare,*
published by the U.S. Department of Health and Human Services

As you can see, each Medigap policy from "C" through "J" offers "skilled nursing care facility" as a benefit. However, this does *not* cover long-term care because Medicare itself does not cover long-term care.

Instead, Medicare pays only for "skilled" care in a nursing home—care that's medically necessary rather than merely custodial. Because Medicare only pays for skilled care, Medigap policies only cover the daily co-payments ($99 per day in 2001) for days 21 through 100, as well as certain home health care expenses.

Even though Medigap policies don't cover custodial care, they still may be essential, especially for clients who are in traditional Medicare rather than in a Medicare HMO. Therefore, you probably should become knowledgeable about the coverage that's offered in your area.

Among Medigap policies, which ones make the most sense? For basic coverage, "A" is by far the least expensive. These policies must cover the co-payments of $198 per day (in 2001) for hospital days 61 through 90, $396 for a further 60 "lifetime reserve days," and full payments for another 365 days. They also must pay the 20% co-insurance amounts for medical expenses —especially doctors' bills—that Medicare requires from patients. The first three units of blood or blood components not covered by Medicare also are included in these core policies. If affordability is an issue for your clients, Policy "A" provides protection against disastrous expenses.

> **If affordability is an issue for your clients, Policy "A" provides protection against disastrous expenses.**

Many clients will prefer more extensive—and more expensive—coverage. Beyond the basic benefits, you can help them decide which features are worth paying for. If they travel out of the country frequently, they might want to buy a policy with this coverage; if they anticipate spending a great deal on prescription drugs, there are three policies that offer some coverage.

Policy "F," which is among the more popular choices, costs more than twice as much as the "A" policies but it offers coverage for skilled nursing co-payments, foreign health emergencies, and excess doctors' charges. Policy "I" offers the same benefits as well as prescription drug coverage so it's a good buy for people who expect to pay $700 or more per year for drugs.

Recommendation: Clients who have health problems may want to buy Medigap insurance when they first receive medical coverage under Medicare, generally at age 65. Normally, applicants with health conditions will have a difficult time buying health insurance. However, under federal law there's a six-month "window" following

> **There's a six-month "window" following someone's 65th birthday. During this period a Medigap insurer must sell all applicants any policy, unconditionally, at the standard premium rate.**

someone's 65th birthday or later enrollment in Medicare Part B. During this period a Medigap insurer must sell all applicants any policy, unconditionally, at the standard premium rate.

Therefore, in that six-month period clients can buy a Medigap policy that pays for prescription drugs, even if it is certain they'll be using a great deal of expensive medication each year. (The insurer can exclude coverage for a preexisting condition for up to six months.) After that six-month window, they may not be able to buy the Medigap policy of their choice at the best price.

Thus, it's important to keep an eye out for a client's 65th birthday, especially if he or she is now covered by hospital-surgical, major medical or comprehensive health insurance. If that coverage ends on the client's 65th birthday, you might suggest converting it to a Medigap policy. That will mean no wait for coverage of existing problems already approved for that policy.

For example, a client can buy a top-of-the-line Policy "J" even with a health condition that makes it certain he or she will need extensive care in the future. Policy "J" offers prescription drug coverage up to $3,000 per year.

Dizzying Differences

Standardized policies haven't brought standardized premiums. Indeed, rates vary greatly from company to company in the same location. In the same city, a 65-year-old man might pay less than $500 per year for Policy "A" from one insurer and more than $1,000 a year from another. Plan "J" might cost that man $1,700 from one company and over $3,000 per year from another.

Why are there such great disparities? In some cases, high premiums are caused by marketing strategies: companies don't want to sell a certain policy in a certain area, or they'll sell it only at a very high price. Other differences include the way premiums change as consumers age, insurers' underwriting policies, and their financial strength.

In essence, Medigap policies are either "age-rated" or "community-rated." Further, those that are age-rated may use an "issue age" or "attained age" approach.

- **Issue age**. With this type of policy, policyholders pay a level premium that's determined by the age at which they first buy the policy. If the company wants to raise the premium, it has to raise the premiums of everyone else in that area holding similar policies.

- **Attained age**. With this method, clients pay relatively low initial premiums that increase as they grow older.

  Either way, an age-rated system results in lower premiums for younger buyers.

- **Community rating**. This method, in which a company charges the same rates for everyone, regardless of age, benefits older consumers at the expense of younger ones. Thus, it may be a good buy for clients who are over 75 years of age.

Another factor that sets some companies apart is their screening procedures. Some Medigap insurers offer guaranteed access to policies "A" through "G," without using medical underwriting to screen applicants. Other insurers underwrite plans "A" through "G," meaning that they deny coverage to some applicants. Most companies use medical underwriting for plans "H," "I," and "J" because they offer prescription drug benefits.

Thus, clients should shop around before buying Medigap insurance. What's more, you should find out what method the company is using to price its policies so you can tell clients what to expect in the future. When comparing prices of Medigap policies, consider the total cost for the next five or 10 years, not just one year; make sure clients ask for discounts for couples or nonsmokers, which may help bring premiums down.

Chapter 4

MEDICAID PLANNING
Pleading Poverty

The previous chapters have made it clear that neither Medicare nor Medigap insurance provides much coverage for LTC. By default, Medicaid has become "nursing home insurance" for many Americans. If someone is poor — with few assets and little income — he can qualify for Medicaid, a federal-state welfare program. Then, Medicaid will pay for LTC in a nursing home.

Moreover, some middle-class Americans become "artificially poor" in order to qualify for Medicaid. They transfer nearly all of their assets to family members, then apply for Medicaid as poverty cases.

Wait Limits

Qualifying for Medicaid is no easy matter. Medicaid applicants have to report current assets as well as a history of asset transfers (gifts, below-market sales) within the previous 36 months. For transfers to trusts, applicants must provide a report that goes back 60 months.

Therefore, if your clients transfer assets and wait 36 months, they can apply for Medicaid without worrying. There will be nothing to report and no problems qualifying, assuming their assets are below the poverty line. (If they transfer assets to a trust, they'll have to wait for 60 months before applying.)

In some cases, the waiting period needn't be 36 or 60 months. There may be a shorter wait, depending on a simple formula.

Suppose, for example, you practice in an area where nursing home costs average $6,000 per month. After giving away $150,000, a client would be eligible for Medicaid following a 25-month wait ($150,000 divided by $6,000). If the nursing home average costs had been $5,000 per month, the waiting period would have been 30 months.

The catch? If someone applies before the appropriate waiting period ends, the application will be denied. In some cases, applying too early can stretch out the mandatory waiting period.

Bare Essentials

> At the time you apply for Medicaid, you can have only a certain amount of assets — essentially, a house, a car, some personal jewelry, and a few thousand dollars in the bank.

Of course, there's more to qualifying for Medicaid than transferring assets and waiting for a certain number of months. At the time you apply, you can have only a certain amount of assets: essentially, a house, a car, some personal jewelry, and a few thousand dollars in the bank.

Does it make sense to advise a client to go into poverty just so Medicaid will pay any future nursing home bills? Not if that client is relatively young and healthy. After such a transfer, the person giving away the assets is dependent upon the goodwill of the recipient.

However, as clients grow older they are more likely to need nursing home care. At some point, they might consider transferring assets to loved ones and applying for Medicaid once the waiting period is over. Then, Medicaid will pay any nursing home bills. (If a client has to go into a nursing home sooner, it's up to someone else to pay the expenses. Thus, clients who choose asset giveaways had better choose recipients carefully.)

Keep in mind that transferring assets from one spouse to another may not work because one spouse can't have more than a certain amount of assets (about $85,000 in 2001) in order for the other spouse to qualify for Medicaid. Often, Medicaid transfers are made to grown sons or daughters.

If you think an asset transfer is a possibility, perhaps in the future, be sure that your client's estate plan includes powers of attorney or a revocable trust (see Chapter 7). In case your client become incapacitated, an agent or successor trustee can handle the asset transfers in your place.

Time for Trusts

Rather than making outright gifts, are you better off transferring assets to a trust? Usually not. Trusts are expensive and the waiting period may be longer. However, there are some circumstances in which trusts may be appropriate:

• Your clients are not comfortable making outright gifts. Their children may be spendthrifts or in marriages that seem destined for divorce. The parents may prefer to put assets into the hands of a reliable trustee.

• Clients want to provide for a loved one with special needs. Outright gifts may not be prudent while a trust may provide long-term security.

What's more, gifts to a disabled child or a trust created for that child's benefit don't count as transfers for the purpose of determining Medicaid eligibility. A client can make such a transfer today and apply for Medicaid tomorrow.

Who counts as a disabled child? He or she must meet Social Security's definition of disability: not able to do meaningful amounts of work because of a physical or mental condition.

Another planning opportunity is available to people under 65 who meet this criterion for disability. If someone else (perhaps a parent) creates a trust, the disabled person can transfer all of his or her assets to the trust and immediately qualify for Medicaid.

Then, a friendly trustee can make distributions on behalf of the disabled person from this "special needs" trust. This money can supplement Medicaid, providing extras (clothing, favored foods, show tickets) not offered by public assistance.

It's true the trust must completely reimburse Medicaid, after the disabled person's death, before anyone else can inherit. Often, the entire trust fund will go to Medicaid. However, Medicaid would have gotten the money anyway; this special needs trust can enhance the disabled person's quality of life.

Estates Owe Medicare: Assets at Risk

In the list of assets permitted Medicaid recipients, you may have noticed some loopholes. Someone can have a house or a car of any value and still qualify for Medicaid.

> **After a nursing home patient dies, states are able to collect from their estates the money that Medicaid paid for LTC.**

Recent changes in federal and state laws have led to a crackdown. Now, after a nursing home patient dies, states are able to collect from their estates the money that Medicaid paid for LTC. In practice, this means that Medicaid can place a lien on the family home, if Medicaid is paying the nursing home bills. After the resident's death, or the death of the spouse, Medicaid can collect the money due from sale proceeds.

Thus, a client may think that he's leaving a house worth $200,000 to his children. In reality, Medicaid will take its cut first, leaving only $150,000 or $100,000 or even nothing for the heirs.

Poor Choices

Now that you understand the ground rules of Medicaid, you can see why it doesn't pay to count on this source to pay for LTC, especially for nursing home bills.

OPTION 1. A client spends all of his money on LTC and then applies for Medicaid. If this happens, your client won't leave any legacy.

OPTION 2. A client gives away all of his money to children or other loved ones, assuring an "inheritance" for those heirs. However, that means your client won't have enough money to support himself, so he'll become dependent on others.

If your client never needs LTC, he will have impoverished himself for no reason. If he does need LTC, he'll have to rely upon someone else to pay the bills until the waiting period is over and he's eligible for Medicaid.

OPTION 3. A client gives away all of his money to a trust. As mentioned above, there may be good reasons for such a move. However, this strategy requires a skilled attorney, incurs legal fees, extends the waiting period for Medicaid and still leaves the client dependent on others.

As you can see, none of these options is particularly appealing. You might prefer to suggest another option, the purchase of a specialized insurance policy to cover LTC, as explained in Chapter 5. With this insurance, clients can retain their independence *and* leave a legacy.

Nevertheless, there are situations in which some Medicaid planning is appropriate:

• Your client may be too old or too ill to buy LTC insurance.

• Income may not be sufficient to cover the premiums.

• Your client may have a younger, healthier relative that can be trusted to provide care after an asset transfer.

• There may be special family situations that make Medicaid planning desirable.

If it seems advisable to go ahead with Medicaid planning, advise clients to proceed cautiously, with the advice of a lawyer. Moreover, they should retain a lawyer who's experienced in elder care: call the National Association of Elder Law Attorneys at 520/881-4005 for a local referral. The money paid in legal fees can save a lot of heartaches in the future.

Better Than Nothing

One technique that may be appropriate for some people can be called the "half a loaf is better than none" approach. Suppose, for example, that Jane Brown has $200,000 worth of assets. She's 85 years old, still healthy, but concerned about her future.

She might give $100,000 to her two children and keep the other $100,000. Now, she still has enough assets to live independently, considering the fact that she lives in a mortgage-free condo and has a modest income from Social Security.

What happens if Jane has to go into a nursing home? In her area, the average cost of a nursing home is about $5,000 per month. Thus, she has enough to pay for 20 months. After she has spent down virtually all of her assets she'll be able to apply for Medicaid because the waiting period (her $100,000 transfer divided by the $5,000 average cost) will have elapsed.

In this case, Jane will have assured herself that half of her wealth — $100,000 — winds up with her loved ones, rather than in the pockets of a nursing-home operator. Of course, if she never needs to be institutionalized, the other $100,000 can be left to her children.

It is essential for clients to have a power of attorney or living trust in place.

Note that this strategy can work if Jane falls down some steps, for example, and goes into a nursing home unexpectedly, with no realistic prospect of ever living independently again. She can transfer half of her wealth to her children, spend down the other half in the nursing home, and then apply for Medicaid.

However, such last-minute planning won't be possible if she has a stroke or some other condition that prevents her from making transfers. That's why it is essential for clients to have a power of attorney or living trust in place, as explained in Chapter 7.

Again, you probably should not advocate Medicaid planning (that is, asset transfers) if other strategies are available. If nothing else can help your clients, though, they can turn to Medicaid, but they should work with a savvy professional to make sure that everything is done properly.

Massaging the Medicaid Rules

If you or a loved one are forced to depend on Medicaid, you might as well make the most of the rules. For example, there are limits on how much you or your spouse can have, in terms of assets, in order to qualify for Medicaid. On the other hand, some states don't impose income limits. In that case, it may make sense to convert disqualifying assets to a disregarded income stream: you can do so by buying an immediate annuity.

With an immediate annuity, a client gives money to an insurance company, which promises a lifetime payout. In return for a somewhat lower monthly payout, the insurer will guarantee the annuity for a "period certain," a minimum number of years. Then, if the primary recipient dies before the period certain expires, a beneficiary will receive the outstanding payments.

As far as Medicaid is concerned, buying an immediate annuity is not the same as making a gift or selling assets below their fair value. Thus, buying an immediate annuity won't cause a waiting period for Medicaid eligibility. (This is true only if the period certain is the same period or less than the annuitant's life expectancy; choosing a longer period will be considered a transfer to the beneficiary.)

To see how an immediate annuity can help with LTC, consider the case of an elderly couple, Saul and Helen Taylor. Saul is in a nursing home, rapidly depleting their assets. Their best option is to qualify Saul for Medicaid, but the couple has about $200,000 in assets, over the Medicaid limit.

Here's a strategy they should consider:

1. **Transfer all of the couple's assets to Helen.** Asset transfers between spouses don't generate a Medicaid waiting period.

   Now, Saul has no assets so he's under the Medicaid limits. However, Helen has $200,000, while she's only allowed $85,000, in 2001.

2. **Helen buys an immediate annuity.** She spends $115,000 on the annuity, which drops her assets to $85,000 and enables Saul to qualify for Medicaid without any waiting period.

The amount of the annuity Helen will receive depends on several factors. Assume that she is 83 years old, she wants a seven-year period certain annuity, and interest rates are about the level of early 2001.

In these circumstances, Helen might receive around $1,200 per month, or $14,400 per year, and nearly all of her payments will be a tax-free return of capital, for the first seven years.

She'll receive those payments as long as she lives. If she dies after, say, three years, her designated beneficiaries (their children, in this example) will receive four more years of payments from the insurance company.

The advantages of this arrangement are obvious. Medicaid picks up the nursing home bill while Helen gets a steady income stream for the rest of her life. She'll receive a substantial income stream, too; the older you are when you buy an immediate annuity, the greater the monthly cash flow, as a percentage of your investment.

The disadvantage? After seven years there are no more guaranteed payments. When Helen dies, the cash flow dies, too. There will be nothing from that initial $115,000 payment for the children to inherit.

> **Immediate annuities work best if ongoing cash flow is more important than a future inheritance.**

Thus, immediate annuities work best if ongoing cash flow is more important than a future inheritance. If your client is interested, help him or her get bids from several insurers, because the amounts they'll pay may differ.

Miller Trusts

The immediate annuity strategy outlined above can work for single people, too. Gail Campbell, age 78, might liquidate her assets to purchase an immediate annuity. As long as she does not choose a period certain annuity with a term extending beyond her life expectancy (about 10 years for Gail), she won't have to report any transfers and won't have a waiting period before applying for Medicaid.

Then, if Gail goes into an LTC facility, relying on Medicaid to pay the bills, she probably will have to turn over her annuity checks to the facility along with her Social Security checks and any other income, retaining only a small "personal needs allowance."

Her immediate annuities raise other issues, though. There are "income caps" on certain public assistance programs; in some states, Medicaid is subject to income caps, perhaps around $1,500 per month. If her annuity income places her over the limit, she won't qualify.

The same problem is faced by Medicaid applicants who have large Social Security or pension income they can't disclaim. This is a real Catch-22 for some people: they don't have enough wealth to afford a nursing home stay; yet, they have an unstoppable stream of income that disqualifies them from Medicaid.

Fortunately, there may be a solution. In many situations it's possible to set up a "Miller trust" to hold the excess income and enable the recipient to qualify for public assistance. Suppose, for example, that Gail's annuity income, Social Security benefits, and pension income add up to $1,700 per month yet her state permits Medicaid recipients to have no more than $1,500 per month in income.

Working with an experienced attorney, she can establish a Miller trust to hold the excess $200 per month. Ultimately—probably at her death—the money that has accumulated in this trust will go to the government agencies that have subsidized her care. In the meantime, Medicaid will pay her nursing home bills.

Home Field Advantage: Home Assets

> A life estate permits the buyer to live in the house as long as he or she lives.

Medicaid applicants may face income limits but there's generally no restrictions on home ownership, which may open up some planning possibilities. A client might, for example, pay off a mortgage, moving assets from cash or securities (which will prevent Medicaid eligibility) into home equity (which won't). However, as mentioned above, states that have paid for LTC through Medicaid may eventually recover those outlays from the home equity.

A more attractive strategy may be available to the elderly who no longer own a home, or who never owned one. They can use liquid assets to purchase a "life estate" in a house owned by a loved one, perhaps a son or daughter. A life estate permits the buyer to live in the house as long as he or she lives. As long as the value of the life estate (actuarially determined by the federal government) is no less than the amount that's paid, no transfer will have occurred, for Medicaid reporting purposes, and no waiting period will be incurred.

This strategy permits the elderly to move assets to younger relatives without incurring a Medicaid penalty. It's not necessary that the buyer actually live in the house—she might be staying in a nursing home —but the life estate will count as a "home," exempt from Medicaid's list of forbidden assets.

Again, with all of these Medicaid planning tactics it's critical that you insist that your clients act under the advice of a lawyer who knows this subject thoroughly.

Emergency LTC Planning

Advise clients in this situation to start by hiring a lawyer, preferably a well-regarded attorney who specializes in what's known as "elder law." State laws vary widely so it's critical to hire someone who's knowledgeable about the local situation.

In an ideal world, your clients would spend as much time planning for LTC as they do for a trip to Florida. Everyone would have a power of attorney in place, assets held in trust, a solid LTC insurance policy, and so on.

Unfortunately, we don't live in such a world. For many clients, planning for LTC is something to do tomorrow. However, tomorrow never comes and suddenly someone in the family needs LTC today. Then it's too late for planning.

If this should happen—if your client or a loved one needs to go into a nursing home and no preparations have been made—what can be done?

Advise clients in this situation to start by hiring a lawyer, preferably a well-regarded attorney who specializes in what's known as "elder law." State laws vary widely so it's critical to hire someone who's knowledgeable about the local situation.

Even though you don't practice law, here are some strategies you might suggest when clients find themselves in an emergency LTC situation:

- **Get the person who needs LTC admitted to a first-rate nursing home**. There is a tremendous difference in quality among these institutions: some are truly fodder for tabloid TV, while others are staffed by caring individuals. Naturally, the better ones are expensive and well-occupied but you should make every effort to help your client gain admission to a top-of-the-line home.

Many of the better homes discourage or even refuse to admit Medicaid patients because reimbursement rates are low. Therefore, you'll probably want your client to enter the nursing home as a paying customer. Later, if a Medicaid application is accepted, nursing homes tend to keep their patients rather than evict them.

- **If Medicaid seems like a solution, arrange an asset giveaway**. The trick here is for the nursing home resident to keep enough assets to pay nursing home bills until the Medicaid waiting period expires.

  For example, if a client has $100,000 in assets, she might give away $70,000 to her children while keeping $30,000. Assume that the average cost of a nursing home in her area is $5,000; she can apply for Medicaid after a 14-month waiting period ($70,000 divided by $5,000).

  During those 14 months, she can spend down her $30,000 on nursing home payments. The shortfall can be covered by her income (from Social Security, for example), and perhaps by contributions from other family members. Even if the family has to kick in $25,000 over that 14-month period, they'll still wind up ahead. After the 14 months are up, your client can apply for Medicaid, which will pay her ongoing nursing home bills.

- **Married couples need to plan for two**. Some states allow the so-called "community spouse" (the one who does not need to be in a nursing home) to have about $85,000 worth of assets (in 2001) while the other spouse is covered by Medicaid. Thus, assets can be structured so that the community spouse has the protected $85,000, other assets are given away, and the institutionalized spouse has enough assets to pay for the nursing home during the waiting period.

  In some states that $85,000 serves as a minimum as well as a maximum. Other states, though, allow the community spouse to keep *half* of the marital assets, up to $85,000. If the couple has $120,000 for example, the community spouse is allowed to keep only $60,000, not $85,000.

In the above example, what happens to the "excess" $60,000?

- It can be given away, triggering a Medicaid waiting period.

- It can be spent down on nursing home costs until the couple meets the Medicaid rules.

- It can be used to buy assets that are exempt from Medicaid. The money can be used to pay off a mortgage, perhaps, or to buy a prepaid funeral.

- It can remain the property of the community spouse, who dares Medicaid to sue. This is a "hardball" strategy that will appeal to some clients, but not others. In some states, Medicaid will negotiate with the community spouse in these situations, perhaps requiring a token payment as the price of staying out of court. A savvy lawyer can help you decide if this last option is viable.

Chapter 5

LONG-TERM CARE INSURANCE
An Increasingly Popular Solution to an Age-Old Problem

Medicaid is not an ideal solution for LTC, as the previous chapters have illustrated. Nevertheless, some kind of a plan is necessary to help your clients deal with the expense of LTC. Such an outlay can be substantial and permanent — it's not the same as a stock market correction and a rebound that's likely to follow.

One way to plan for LTC is to help clients get rich. With $1 million or $2 million in investment assets, clients may not need to insure against a possible $50,000 or even a $90,000 annual nursing-home bill.

Thus, wealthy people can self-insure. However, even for those clients who fall into that category, accumulating wealth shouldn't be the end of their plan. In case LTC is needed, people who self-insure may have to liquidate assets. Which assets should be liquidated? The stocks or the bonds? Who'll make the decision? You, or the client, or another family member?

Even if there are ample assets, the process of paying for LTC can be very stressful for your clients. After considering everything, they may decide to buy LTC insurance from a sound company, to preserve peace of mind as well as the family fortune.

Moreover, not everyone will be in a position to pay for a long nursing-home stay out of current cash flow. Clients who wind up with $300,000, or $500,000, or even $1 million in investment assets may find it difficult to carry the expense, if it becomes necessary. Such people — those who are in the middle, neither rich nor poor — may be good candidates for LTC insurance.

Moreover, don't let clients be misled if they have $1 million, or even more, in a 401(k), IRA, or other tax-deferred retirement plan. That's pretax money, not "real," spendable cash. To use this money they'll have to withdraw it and pay income tax. In order to get their hands on $60,000, for example, they'll probably have to withdraw about $100,000 — and their retirement fund will swiftly shrink.

Comfort Zone

Long-term care insurance is bought for emotional as well as financial reasons.

Faced with such realities, people are increasingly buying LTC insurance. Reportedly, growth in LTC coverage has been expanding by 25%-30% per year.

Therefore, LTC insurance is a solution that will appeal to many clients. Moreover, LTC insurance is bought for emotional as well as financial reasons. Even if LTC insurance isn't needed, strictly going by the numbers, clients may prefer to buy the insurance anyway, just for the security of knowing they won't be a burden for their children, even if they need extended care.

Some clients appreciate the need for LTC insurance more than others. Generally, men may not be as receptive to the idea of LTC insurance, tending to downplay the need for this coverage. At the same time, women may be more interested because they know who will bear the burden of caring for someone who needs constant attention.

The more middle-aged people have to care for aging relatives, the more they realize what a burden it can be. Even if they have the money to pay for care, at home or in a facility, they may not have the time to figure out what care is needed and monitor it regularly. Increasingly, insurance companies are including care coordination with LTC policies, which is a major benefit. They're presenting these policies as a way to preserve a lifestyle.

Therefore, the clients who are most likely to buy LTC insurance are those who have seen an elderly relative go through a long, expensive bout of institutional care. They've seen how stressful it can be, so they want the insurance, in some cases regardless of the price.

Feature Attractions

Most clients, though, will not be cost-insensitive; indeed, affordability is a key issue for many potential buyers of LTC insurance. That's true even though insurers claim that premiums have fallen in recent years. LTC insurance is still pricey, especially when a retired couple, living on a fixed income, decides to buy two policies.

Advise clients to shop carefully for LTC insurance because premiums can vary considerably. For example, a 65-year-old man might buy a policy paying $100 per day, for up to four years, for $850 per year from Insurer A, while a similar policy from Insurer B, sold in the same city, might cost $1,350 per year, or about 60% more.

For married couples, both spouses should buy policies from the same company. Typically, discounts ranging up to 20% are available.

In order to help clients shop among LTC policies you need to know how they're structured. Generally, an LTC policy will have the following features:

- **Daily benefits**. Most LTC policies pay a certain amount per day if the insured individual needs LTC. Benefits might range from $50 per day (about $18,000 per year) to $300 per day (over $100,000 per year).

- **Elimination period**. This is the waiting period before benefits begin. With a 20-day elimination period, for example, a policy-holder is obligated to pay the first 20 days of LTC out of his own pocket. Naturally, the shorter the waiting period the more expensive the policy will be.

- **Benefit period**. Once benefits begin, how long will they continue? The most expensive policies provide lifetime benefits while others limit benefits to 2, 3, 4, 5, or 6 years.

- **Inflation adjustment rider**. If you buy a policy with a $100 daily benefit in 2001, that $100 might not buy much LTC in 2011 or 2021. Therefore, some policies will increase the benefit by, say, 5% per year (simple or compounded). This feature is expensive but it's probably worth it for clients who buy the policy while they're in their 60s, many years in advance of probable need.

- **Care alternatives**. LTC insurance should not be merely "nursing home" insurance. You should recommend policies that will provide care under any or all of the following circumstances:

Home care. If a client needs a qualified caregiver to come to the home, the policy should provide coverage.

Adult day-care center. The policy should explicitly include these types of facilities, where clients spend part of a day, yet go home at night.

Assisted-living facilities. As described previously, this term describes living arrangements in which some services (meals, laundry, medication, reminders) are available; but residents still live independently within the complex. A good-quality LTC policy will pay a benefit if policyholders reside in such a facility.

Nursing homes. These are institutions for people who no longer can care for themselves, so they need constant attention. Clients' greatest LTC financial exposure comes from a long nursing-home stay, so be sure they have this coverage.

You should be aware that some insurers try to push "home care" policies as a means of allowing the elderly to stay out of a nursing home. In truth, no insurance policy will accomplish this if someone truly needs that level of institutionalization. If a client is going to buy an LTC policy, make sure it covers nursing-home stays.

Cost Cutters

How much might LTC insurance cost? A 70-year-old who buys a policy with a $100 daily benefit ($36,500 per year) and a three-year benefit period (a maximum of $110,000 in benefits, before inflation adjustments) might pay anywhere from $1,700 to $3,000 per year, depending on specific policy features. If a married couple needs this coverage, the cost would be doubled, or nearly so. (Many companies offer a 10%-20% discount on dual purchases by married couples.) Not every retired couple can afford to shell out $3,400 to $6,000 per year for LTC insurance.

If affordability is a problem, how can you help clients trim the cost and still acquire adequate coverage?

Advise them to buy when they're relatively young and healthy.

To trim the cost of LTC insurance:
- Advise them to buy when they're relatively young and healthy.
- Don't overinsure.
- Buy a reimbursement policy.

The younger the buyer, the lower the premiums. Nevertheless, it may not make sense to buy when clients are very young and probably many years from a nursing home.

Does that mean it pays to wait to think about LTC insurance? Not really. If clients wait until too late, the premiums can be extremely expensive.

Although LTC insurance may be purchased in the early 50s, when buyers can lock in attractive rates, it's common that purchases aren't made until the buyers are in their 60s. That's when they have some cash to spend, after the kids are through with school and the mortgage has been paid off, and that's when they start thinking about LTC.

Generally, the late 50s to the early 60s are a good age to buy this coverage. At age 60, for example, LTC policies comparable to the one described above might be bought for $1,000-$1,700 per year, slightly more than half the price of coverage if bought at age 70. Even factoring in a time value for the earlier payments, clients get a better deal by buying sooner rather than later. Long term, it's less expensive to buy early and clients will have additional years of coverage.

It's true that these costs really aren't locked in: premiums can be raised in the future. In reality, though, this risk isn't as severe as you might think. Any premium increases have to be across-the-board, for all holders of a given policy, and approved by state regulators. Insurers are not going to rush into this sort of price hike, which can cost a great deal of business—and the price increases might not be approved, at least not in full.

Don't overinsure.

Suppose, in your area, the average cost of a nursing home is $55,000 per year, around $150 per day. Your clients don't have to buy a policy that will pay a benefit of $150 per day.

Instead, they might buy a policy with a lower benefit, say $100 per day, which will be considerably less expensive. In such cases, they're effectively agreeing to coinsure, paying perhaps $50 per day ($1,500 per month) in addition to the insurance benefit. As long as they have income from other sources (investments, Social Security), they may prefer to buy a partial rather than a complete insurance benefit. By saving on the daily benefit, they might be able to buy a longer benefit period, thus providing more catastrophic coverage.

That is, they might buy a policy that will keep paying if they stay in a nursing home five or six years, rather than a policy with a two- or three-year benefit period. Policies with longer benefit periods are more expensive, but clients might be able to afford such coverage by cutting back on the daily benefit.

Buy a reimbursement policy.

Indemnity policies might be considered the traditional LTC policy: a consumer buys a policy that will pay a daily benefit of, say, $100 per day if the consumer needs care. (This need usually is determined when an individual cannot perform certain "activities of daily living" or suffers from failing mental capabilities.) Once the need is certified and the individual receives care, the policy would pay the stated benefit of $100 per day, perhaps increased by an inflation adjustment.

Recently, such policies have been giving way to reimbursement policies, which look less like fixed-payment disability income policies and more like health insurance coverage. At some companies, if this choice is taken and home health care is provided by a licensed professional, the policy will pay the cost of that professional's services, at the going rate.

Reimbursement policies generally are more affordable. Thus, buyers might be able to purchase a greater benefit for the same premium dollars. Some companies that offer this choice report that about 70% of their buyers have selected the reimbursement option.

Weighing the Waiting Period

What about increasing the waiting period before benefits begin, to cut premiums? Clients may not want to go beyond 20 days' waiting period. With Medicare cutting back, people will increasingly go into nursing homes to recover from medical procedures. With a 20-day waiting period, clients might get some coverage, which they wouldn't get from a 100-day waiting period. If they're going to be paying premiums on an LTC policy for years, they'll want to get some benefits, even for short-term stays.

Moreover, going from a 20- to a 90- or 100-day "elimination" period won't save that much in premiums.

What if the policy still is not affordable, even with a reduced daily benefit and a 20-day waiting period? As a rule of thumb, clients shouldn't pay more than 10% of their income for LTC insurance. If they would have to exceed that limit, they might not be good candidates for LTC insurance. In that case, you might suggest they see a lawyer about Medicaid planning.

> **As a rule of thumb, clients shouldn't pay more than 10% of their income for LTC insurance.**

Creative Financing

If clients really desire LTC insurance but lack the income to pay the premiums, there may be other ways to come up with the cash to pay for LTC premiums:

- **Reverse mortgages**. In this arrangement, an elderly homeowner borrows against a paid-up house while still living in it. The money thus obtained is used to buy insurance against the event of a stay in a nursing home.

- **Family support**. Middle-aged children may be willing or even eager to pay LTC premiums on behalf of elderly parents. Vic and Wendy Foster, for example, have four middle-aged children, each of whom pays $1,000 per year towards LTC insurance for their parents. The $4,000 per year covers both Vic and Wendy.

With such an approach, the children are insuring their inheritance, which won't be drained by a long nursing-home stay. The children who help to buy LTC insurance know they won't have to pay nursing home bills in case their parents are institutionalized. In addition, the children know that their parents will be cared for—without the children having to become caregivers.

In fact, with substantial LTC insurance, care in top nursing homes will be available. Some of the best institutions don't accept Medicaid patients because reimbursement rates are low.

Key Points

Although finding an affordable LTC policy is important, that should not be your only criteria when you're helping clients to shop for coverage. What else should you keep in mind?

- **Financial strength**. Look for a sizable, well-established insurance company. Clients might need to collect benefits 10, 20, or 30 years from now, so they'll want an insurer that's likely to have staying power.

- **Benefit triggers**. What events have to occur in order for policy-holders collect benefits?

A solid LTC policy will pay if someone has difficulty performing two or more activities of daily living, or ADLs. The more ADLs listed on the policy, the more likely someone can qualify for benefits. Here are the ADLs a policy should list:
    Dressing
    Eating
    Bathing
    Mobility (getting in and out of chairs, for example)
    Using the toilet
    Continence

In addition, you should not buy an LTC policy unless it specifically provides coverage in case of cognitive impairment such as Alzheimer's or senile dementia.

- **Care coordination**. Some insurers have experts who'll help family members plan for LTC.

- **Alternate plans of care**. In some instances the insurer will suggest home modifications, medical equipment, and home response systems as an alternative to institutionalization. Rehabilitation programs also may be offered.

- **Bed reservation**. If a policyholder must move from an LTC facility to a hospital, some LTC insurance policies will pay any amounts necessary to keep a bed reserved, upon discharge from the hospital.

- **Respite care**. Before the insurance policy's waiting period has been satisfied, a family member or paid caregiver may have to provide LTC. Some LTC policies will pay to provide such caregivers some temporary relief.

- **Waiver of premiums**. If a policyholder is receiving benefits, the premium payments will be suspended, with this feature.

When a client is shopping for LTC insurance, see if these features are present. The same holds true if an employer gives a client the option of buying into an LTC insurance group plan. Check the policy that's offered carefully to see how the coverage and costs compare with what the client can buy individually.

Long-Term Shortcomings

If you're helping clients find LTC insurance, read the policies carefully. Look for tip-offs to the quality of the contract.

For example, see what has to be done in order to meet the "waiting period" requirement so benefits will be paid.

- **Good policy**. The policyholder must satisfy the waiting period only once while the policy is in force. There is no requirement for consecutive days of care and no limited period in which the days of the waiting period must occur.

- **Inferior policy**. Days of long-term care count towards the waiting period only if they are consecutive or if they occur within a certain time period. Thus, a policyholder may have to satisfy the waiting period several times in order for benefits to begin.

Taxing Matters

Another subject needs to be considered when shopping for LTC insurance: taxation. Congress is so determined that individuals (not government agencies) will bear the burden of LTC, that it has created tax incentives to encourage people to buy LTC insurance. People who have LTC insurance won't have to rely on Medicaid, the federal-state welfare system that now pays most of the nation's nursing home bills.

Therefore, the Health Insurance Portability and Accountability Act (HIPAA) of 1996 divided the world of LTC insurance into two types of policies, tax-qualified and nonqualified. The policies that comply with HIPAA are "tax-qualified," offering two major benefits.

- First, premiums may be deductible, up to certain limits, depending on the age of the insured individual.

Age Before Year-End Maximum Deduction
For LTC Insurance Premiums in 2001

40 or under	$ 230
41-50	$ 430
51-60	$ 860
61-70	$2,290
71+	$2,860

- Second, benefits received under tax-qualified LTC policies generally will not be taxable.

In order to qualify for these tax benefits, LTC policies must meet certain standards. The insured individual must be unable to perform at least two of these ADLs: eating, bathing, dressing, getting out of bed, using the toilet, and continence. Moreover, a licensed health-care professional must certify that these conditions will last for at least 90 days. (All LTC policies bought before 1997 were "grandfathered" by HIPAA so they qualify for the two tax breaks listed above.)

In. the marketplace, it appears that tax-qualified policies are crowding out nonqualified policies—reportedly, about 90% of the policies sold now are tax-qualified. The tax benefits are written into law, so there's no question about them. Many clients want tax-qualified policies because that's the only way they can be sure of the tax advantages.

Those clients, though, might not be able to deduct all, or even part, of their LTC premiums, due to complexities in the tax code. However, there are circumstances in which clients may be able to get substantial deductions for LTC insurance.

- Clients who are self-employed can treat the premiums for LTC insurance the same as they treat health insurance premiums, for tax purposes.

  Self-employed individuals can deduct 60% of the premiums they pay for health insurance in 2001, and that portion will escalate to 100% by the year 2003. Similar deductions also may be taken for premiums paid by the self-employed for LTC insurance, subject to the age-based limits mentioned above.

- Clients who are employers may provide LTC insurance benefits to employees, just as they provide health insurance benefits. That is, premiums are deductible for the employer while employees don't have to recognize taxable income.

- Even more tax advantages for LTC insurance may be coming out of Washington soon. It's possible that a new federal law will provide a tax credit or an above-the-line deduction for LTC insurance purchases, to make it easier for people to obtain this coverage.

We also may see legislation that would allow participants to purchase LTC insurance within their 401(k) plans or other retirement accounts. That would be a good fit: as workers build up assets inside retirement plans, this insurance provides a means of protecting those assets.

Qualifying for LTC

Naturally, clients can't expect to buy LTC insurance if they're heading for a nursing home the next day. That's another reason for buying while relatively young: clients are more likely to be in good health so they can get coverage at reasonable rates. In general, insurance companies will screen applicants' health histories and reject those who seem likely to be institutionalized in the near future.

No one company is right for all situations, and price is not necessarily the deciding factor. Tolerance of medical conditions may be even more important. Insurance companies don't all have identical underwriting criteria: some are more tolerant of certain conditions than others. Typically, if clients have been diagnosed with:

- multiple sclerosis
- osteoporosis
- Parkinson's disease
- chronic memory loss

they probably won't be able to purchase LTC insurance. On the other hand, there are insurers who will cover applicants even if they have been treated (successfully) for cancer, have recovered from a heart attack, or recuperated from hip- or knee-replacement surgery. (If clients have serious health problems and their employer offers a group plan with guaranteed coverage, be sure they sign up.)

You and your clients should beware of LTC insurers that practice "back-end underwriting." Such insurance companies accept virtually all applicants, regardless of their health.

What's the catch? If a policyholder goes into a nursing home and files a claim for benefits, these insurers will try to find a pre-existing medical problem that wasn't revealed, in order to deny the claim. Someone who is in a nursing home, mentally or physically weak, probably won't be in any condition to do battle with the insurance company.

Instead, urge clients to buy LTC insurance from a company that does its underwriting when they apply, a company that asks many questions about their health. Policies from such companies are harder to obtain but, once such a company accepts an applicant, he's more likely to collect after filing a claim.

Simplified Solutions

As you can see, helping clients to choose among LTC policies can be complicated. Nevertheless, as the need for LTC insurance increases, distribution channels are expanding. Formerly, most LTC insurance was sold by agents and brokers who were specialists in this area, but now others, such as financial planners, are becoming more involved.

A streamlined underwriting process may make it easier for planners to sell LTC insurance. Some companies use trained nurses to interview applicants by phone. They report better and faster information than they'd get by relying upon the applicants' doctors; this process may take weeks off the time until an application is approved.

Some LTC insurers are attempting to make their policies easier for financial planners to sell. They might offer a modified LTC product line that simplifies policies for planners as well as for consumers: there are fewer choices that have to be made, to reduce complexity.

Such policies might have common features, such as a 30-day waiting period and full benefits for home health care. Varying features might be the daily benefit, length of benefit period, and presence or absence of inflation protection.

The advantage? You don't need to be an LTC specialist to explain these policies to clients. However, you do need to be able to ask the right questions. Rather than merely inquire, "Are you healthy?," you need to get more details about medication, previous hospital visits, and so on, in order to get realistic proposals.

Double Coverage

Some financial planners may prefer to recommend LTC insurance as part of a combination product. Certain variable annuities, for example, allow withdrawals for needed care, free of surrender charges, and provide access to eldercare information, as well as discounts from certain providers.

Such variable annuities may not be adequate as a full LTC solution, but they do provide some protection and increased awareness of insurance as a solution to LTC. A discussion of the annuity's benefits may eventually lead to the sale of a stand-alone LTC policy. These hybrid products may appeal to young people, those in their early 30s to mid-50s, and introduce them to the idea of LTC insurance.

With other variable annuities, clients can receive a monthly benefit equal to a certain percentage of the initial investment in case care is needed. Such a feature might have no medical requirements, but a lengthy waiting period.

Research shows that people have two major concerns as they grow older: outliving their income and having to cope with increasing health-care costs. LTC insurance could help them address one of those issues, but there has been resistance to buying. Consumers don't like the use-it-or-lose-it aspect of these premiums — they'll never collect any benefits if they don't need care — and they're worried about having to pay rising premiums after they stop earning income.

Hybrid products may be able to bridge the gap. The variable annuity guarantees a return of investment: it can be structured to pay at least the initial investment amount to the buyer or to a beneficiary. By annuitizing the contract, investors can lock in a life-long income stream.

With a single-premium variable annuity/LTC insurance hybrid, clients make one payment for both products.

In addition, LTC insurance can be obtained at the same time. With a single-premium variable annuity/LTC insurance hybrid, clients make one payment for both products. At the time of purchase, an LTC benefit is selected, which might be so many dollars per day.

Once the policy is purchased, the two sides may operate independently. That is, clients can receive both an income from the annuity and LTC benefits at the same time. Receiving one won't dilute the other. Such a variable annuity/LTC hybrid might cost more than other variable annuities without LTC insurance; and, coverage is underwritten so buyers probably need to be fairly healthy.

These innovative features have been added to variable annuities within the last year or so. Other products are likely to appear, offering still more benefits, as the demand for long-term care increases.

LTC Innovations

What other innovations can planners find in LTC insurance? Some policies offer to pay "independent certified caregivers," not just professionals working for a licensed home health care agency. This may be the direction the market is going; it's certainly likely to be popular with policyholders.

That is, many people prefer to receive home care from friends or family members, especially if such care is mainly custodial. Some policies will pay benefits if the caregiver has been certified as a nursing aide, perhaps at a local community college. They pay charges that are reasonable and customary for that area. If the amount we have to pay is less than the daily benefit the policyholder has chosen, the excess remains available for use at a later date.

Other innovations include 10-year rate guarantees and policies that can be paid in full over 10 years. As America ages and demand for LTC insurance increases, insurers probably will continue to offer additional features, in order to stay competitive.

Room to Grow

The bottom line is that LTC insurance is a needed product that should be familiar to anyone offering comprehensive financial planning. Some clients think they're covered by Medicare, or by a medical insurance plan, which usually is not the case. That may be one reason LTC insurance has only a 6% penetration so far.

Shifting the prime age for buying LTC insurance from the 60s to the 50s would involve Baby Boomers and accelerate the market's growth rate. Some estimates put the market for LTC insurance at $30 billion by 2010. In 1997, by comparison, total premium volume was just over $700 million, according to HIAA. So savvy planners can enjoy a slice of this growing pie, even as they provide valuable services to their clients.

If there's a cloud hanging over the growth of LTC insurance, it's publicity about certain companies that have raised rates in recent years, straining the budgets of elderly policyholders. These policies offered low premiums, liberal benefits, and permissive underwriting; so it's no wonder the insurers ran into trouble.

As a result, planners have to be careful about the LTC policies they recommend. You might want to stick to policies from top-rated companies, those with assets in the billions rather than in the millions.

Nevertheless, planners shouldn't automatically shun an insurance company that has raised rates on LTC policies issued 10 to 20 years ago. Back then, few insurers really knew what they were doing in the LTC area. During the 1990s, though, companies learned a lot more about these policies — or they should have. You should consider a premium increase on a policy issued since then to be a warning sign.

Chapter 6

LIFETIME PAYMENTS FROM LIFE INSURANCE

Some people are unwilling, or unable, to pay several thousand dollars per year for LTC insurance that may never be needed. Clients who are in that category may be more interested in buying life insurance with a "convalescent care rider."

Such policies, offered by many life insurers, provide cash payments in case LTC is needed. In some cases, buyers of such policies will have access to eldercare information as well as discounts from certain providers.

The catch? Any benefit payments will reduce the life insurance proceeds. For example, if a client buys a $250,000 life insurance policy but winds up tapping the convalescent care rider for $100,000, the life insurance death benefit will be only $150,000.

If such a client ultimately needs little or no LTC care, the beneficiary would get a substantial death benefit. Therefore, *someone* will get some benefit from all those premium dollars that have been paid.

Typically, a need for life insurance should be in place for such a strategy to work. Suppose, for example, that Ann Green is 50 years old, with a disabled younger brother being cared for by their mother. When their mother dies, Ann will have to provide care for her brother; if her mother needs LTC before she dies, Ann will be responsible for both of them.

Ann's mother is still in good health (she's insurable) so Ann has decided to buy a policy on her mother's life with a convalescent care rider.

As another example, consider 75-year-old Bill Harris. He has a $50,000 certificate of deposit he keeps rolling over, not spending the interest income. Bill decides to use that money to buy a life insurance policy (a "modified endowment contract" bought with a single payment) with an LTC rider.

This policy will either provide Bill with money to pay for LTC, or pay a death benefit to his family, if he doesn't need care. If Bill needs the money for other purposes in the future, he can cash in the policy, pay the tax, and probably wind up with a return comparable to what he would have earned on the CD.

Generally, a life insurance policy with a convalescent care rider can serve as a complement to, rather than a substitute for, a stand-alone LTC policy. Stand-alone LTC policies are expensive, so some buyers may cut back a bit on benefits to cut premiums. If things don't work out perfectly and those clients need some extra dollars for LTC, such a life insurance policy may be able to fill the gap.

Policy Payoff

Even clients with regular life insurance policies (without an LTC rider) may find such policies useful when a need for LTC arises. If a client has a life insurance policy that's no longer needed, abandoning it or cashing it in are possibilities. Another option, though, might have a greater payoff: sell the policy to a buyer who'll keep the policy in force.

Since the 1980s, such transactions have included "viatical" settlements, involving insured individuals with terminal illnesses. (*Viaticum*, in Latin, refers to the provisions furnished to a Roman official going on a journey.)

Recently, the market has expanded to include "lifetime" settlements. In these transactions, policies are bought from individuals who are not terminally ill, but who might die in 10 to 12 years.

Either way, the policyholder gets money upfront, but, at the insured individual's death, the proceeds go to investors rather than to the original beneficiaries.

Viatical Settlements

As might be expected, insurance policies are easiest to sell in case of a terminal illness. With a short life expectancy, the purchase price will be greater, as a percentage of the policy's face value.

For example, suppose Diane Jackson owns a $200,000 insurance policy on her life. If she has a 12-month life expectancy, a buyer might bid $120,000 (60%) for the policy. At her death, the buyer would collect $200,000. Naturally, a thorough investigation of Diane's medical records will precede any sale.

If you're advising a client interested in a viatical settlement, you should know about the tax treatment. Viatical payments made to terminally ill individuals escape federal income tax. Several states also honor this exclusion, which is permitted no matter how the recipient uses the proceeds.

> **Viatical payments made to terminally ill individuals escape federal income tax.**

To qualify for this tax benefit, a physician has to certify that death is reasonably expected within 24 months. The payment must come from a "viatical settlement provider" who'll report the amounts received (by the insured) to the IRS on Form 1099-LTC.

These providers must be licensed in the state where the insured individual resides; in states where viatical companies aren't licensed, providers must comply with standards established by the National Association of Insurance Commissioners (NAIC).

Assuming the client is in poor health, you as the planner may be the one to check into a buyer's credentials before selling, in order to avoid paying tax on the payment.

Lifetime Settlements

Sellers without a terminal illness can expect to receive a lower price, as a percentage of the policy's face value. In this type of transaction, buyers prefer policies covering the life of a person over 65, who has had some health problem.

Suppose Ed King, 66, has been covered by a $1 million "key-person" policy by his company. Ed, who has had a heart attack, is going to retire, so the key-person coverage no longer is necessary. A buyer, after looking at Ed's medical history and estimating his life expectancy, might offer $150,000 for the policy.

Because this is not a viatical settlement, as defined above, the tax treatment will be different. The tax consequences will depend on the amount paid and the seller's basis in the contract, which generally will be the amount of premiums paid.

Here, Ed's company has paid $150,000 in premiums. With a $150,000 purchase price and $150,000 in premiums paid, no taxes will be due. On the other hand, if Ed's company had paid only $100,000 in premiums, taxes will be due on $50,000 of income.

What tax rates will apply to that income? That depends on the nature of the policy.

- **Permanent life insurance**. Such policies (whole-life, universal life, variable life) have a cash value. The difference between the basis and the cash value will be ordinary income, taxed up to 39.6%; any excess qualifies for the bargain 20% rate on capital gains.

  Suppose $100,000 had been paid in premiums, the cash value was $120,000, and the purchase price was $150,000. The first $20,000 will be taxed as ordinary income while the excess $30,000 is a long-term capital gain.

- **Term life insurance**. Such policies have no cash value and it's uncertain whether ordinary income or capital gains rates apply. As a planner, you might ask whether the client's tax preparer is comfortable reporting such income as a capital gain.

Cash Cows

Older sellers with a health condition may receive relatively high amounts for their life insurance policies. Say Frank Larson, 73, was covered by a $1 million permanent life insurance policy. Now that he is divorced and his children are prospering, there is no loved one who needs the protection of life insurance.

Therefore, Frank does not wish to keep paying the premiums. He could turn in the policy for its $300,000 cash value.

Alternatively, he might be able to sell the policy for more money. A buyer, discovering that Frank has had health problems, might project a relatively short life expectancy and offer $500,000 for the policy.

In many permanent life policies, premiums eventually are paid out of the cash value, which declines. The lower the cash value, the greater the advantage of a lifetime settlement.

Such a policy sale may provide needed cash if someone's circumstances change and LTC is needed. Suppose that Grace Martin, 68, suffers a severe head injury in a skiing accident and is mentally impaired. Medical and custodial care bills may be enormous. Fortunately, she's covered by a $1 million term insurance policy, which her family is able to sell for $200,000 that was needed immediately.

Experience Necessary

If such situations arise among your clients, how do you go about selling a life insurance policy?

- **Seek expert advice**. Ask the life insurance agents and brokers you work with whether they have experience in viatical or lifetime settlements. If so, they can help you by asking for bids from several buyers. If not, they might refer you to an experienced individual.

- **Go online**. The Internet may provide information, too. Go to your favorite search engine and enter "viatical settlements" or "lifetime settlements" to get leads.

If you engage someone to help a client sell an insurance policy, be sure that person's fee or commission will be paid by the *buyer*, not by the seller. What's more, if the agent's fee is based on the policy's selling price rather than its face value (death benefit), there's more incentive to negotiate on your client's behalf.

Tips for Sellers

Once negotiations begin, your client likely will have to supply information about his or her medical history. However, getting the requisite medical information is not always easy because physicians' offices are overwhelmed with paperwork. You may have to insist that your client's doctor and staff proceed rapidly, if there's an urgent need.

As your client solicits bids, he may get multiple forms to fill out. You should find out if your client can cut the paperwork and use a form from only one company—sometimes other buyers will accept them.

In addition, encourage clients in these circumstances to retain an attorney early in the process. A lawyer can help structure the transaction so that a client selling an insurance policy receives cash rather than promises.

Chapter 7

INCAPACITY PLANNING
Truly Worst-Case Scenarios

A s mentioned, death and taxes may be life's only certainties, but gradual deterioration rates a high probability.

Consider the situation facing Dan Harris, a middle-aged physician. His father Mike, in his 90s, had an extraordinary career as a top corporate executive. A year ago, though, Dan was talking with his father and noticed that his dad couldn't grasp some financial concepts that should have been simple for him.

Such deterioration may affect your clients, or their parents, at some stage in life. As this condition progresses, they might lose the ability to manage their own affairs. Some bills won't get paid, while others get paid twice; they may make unnecessary purchases or fall victim to shady schemes.

Ellen James, for example, had always been active politically. As she grew older, though, she began to contribute much larger sums, more frequently, until she was giving more than she could afford. Her daughter Marie had to get a restraining order to halt the increasing solicitations.

Taken to extremes, incapacity could leave your clients, or their parents, without heat, light, phone service, or money in the bank. Fortunately, there are steps you can — and should — suggest to help protect your clients and their family members.

Emphasize that they should act immediately. If they wait until they lose the ability to manage their own affairs, a court will have to be petitioned to appoint a guardian and assets may be jeopardized. Such proceedings are expensive, time consuming, exposed to public scrutiny, and they may require the appointed guardian to post a sizable bond.

Safeguards

Execute a durable power of attorney.

A power of attorney is a document that names an agent who can sign checks, pay bills, and make other financial decisions on behalf of the principal. (The power can name more than one agent, stating whether they may act singly or if they must act in concert.) A client might name a spouse as agent and a son or daughter as backup agent.

That is, the spouse would be empowered to sign legal documents on your client's behalf. The power of attorney is "durable," meaning that it will remain in force even if the creator — your client, in this example — becomes incompetent. If something should happen to the spouse, the son or daughter could act as a replacement.

In general, everyone should create a durable power of attorney. Anyone might be in an auto accident, for example, so there should be someone who can act in case of injury.

A durable power of attorney must be notarized but there's no need to have it recorded anywhere. After a client creates a durable power of attorney, be sure to have it updated every year or two. Many banks and brokerage firms won't accept old powers, while some financial institutions require the use of their own power-of-attorney forms. Therefore, your clients should send a copy of your power to every bank, broker, etc., with whom they do business, to see if there's any problem.

In case a client is reluctant to give someone else such authority, the power of attorney can be a "springing" power, meaning it will take effect only if the creator is unable to act on his or her own behalf. As a safeguard, the document might state that the power will go into effect only if the creator is judged incompetent by three doctors, including his personal physician.

Moreover, clients shouldn't limit a power of attorney to their own assets. Many people put assets into their spouse's name for wealth protection or estate tax reduction. In those cases, there's a danger that the spouse will become incapacitated, unable to manage those assets. Thus, both spouses should be covered by powers of attorney.

If your client agrees to sign a power of attorney, who should be named as the agent who exercises control over the assets? It should be one person, not two; decisions on someone else's behalf should not be made by a committee. Generally, the oldest child living close to the client should be named, assuming that child is responsible. Proximity is important — someone living 50 miles away shouldn't be making day-to-day decisions.

Create a revocable "living" trust.

Any trust a client creates while alive is a living trust; revocable trusts are popular because they can be canceled if the creator changes his mind.

The most common reason for creating a revocable trust is to avoid the time and expense of probate. However, a revocable trust can be used for incompetency planning as well. If a client uses a revocable trust, he also should draft a power of attorney, to cover assets not moved into the trust.

Someone who creates a revocable trust usually will want to act as trustee to retain control of the trust assets. A co-trustee should be named, or a successor trustee can be designated to step in if the creator is certified as incompetent by more than one doctor. The back-up trustee might be a spouse, a grown child, even a bank trust department. Then, if it becomes necessary, the co-trustee or successor trustee can take over management of the trust assets. Some banks and brokerage firms that balk at accepting powers of attorney will-

> **In the event of incompetence, the backup trustee can become the primary trustee without a public court battle.**

ingly deal with successor trustees. (A client who creates such a trust should name several layers of backup trustees, in case someone can't serve.)

In the event of incompetence, the backup trustee can become the primary trustee without a public court battle or private family skirmishes. This arrangement turned out to be enormously helpful to Fran Owens, who had a heart attack just before closing on a house sale. She was in intensive care, but her son, the backup trustee, took over and sold the house, which was held in the trust. Without that trust, the deal might have fallen through.

If a client creates a revocable living trust to hold assets as well as a durable power of attorney to take effect in case of incapacity, will the power of attorney cover the assets held in the trust? There is very little case law on this issue so there are no certain answers.

As a practical matter, this won't be a concern if the person who has the power (the "attorney in fact") is the same person who's named as the successor trustee of the revocable trust. That person will control the assets if your client becomes incapacitated.

A problem might arise, though, if your client names different parties or if an institution is named as successor trustee. Then, a situation might arise in which the attorney-in-fact wants access to trust assets but the trustee is reluctant to go along.

As a solution, the trust documents might specify that no one else besides the initial and the successor trustee can make decisions regarding trust assets. Then, the attorney-in-fact can handle assets not transferred into the trust—use the person's checkbook to pay bills, for example—but conflicts can be avoided.

Arrange for automatic transfers.

Not all incapacity planning involves trusts or powers of attorney— some simple actions may help your clients with day-to-day finances.

Suppose, for example, you're concerned about a widowed client who is becoming increasingly forgetful. It's possible to arrange for most of her income (Social Security checks, pension payments, interest, dividends) to be deposited directly into a bank account. In addition, you can arrange for recurring bills to be paid automatically.

Such steps can reduce the risk of the electricity being turned off for nonpayment, for example. However, it's not possible for every bill to be paid automatically, so other measures may be necessary. In some cases, you can arrange for your client's bills to come to a responsible relative.

Alternatively, an aging client might hire someone to pay bills periodically. If your client is still capable, the person who is hired might be the one who writes the checks while your client signs them—that will reduce the risk of giving an outsider access to the client's checkbook.

Hold some assets in joint ownership.

Another strategy that's relatively simple to implement is to move a client's assets into joint ownership. He might put his name onto a joint bank account with a grown child; then the child can write checks if the parent becomes incapacitated.

Such a tactic is common because it's inexpensive and easy to implement, but there also may be negative aspects to joint ownership. In such arrangements, the surviving co-owner always inherits. That is, if a client changes her brokerage account to joint name, with her son as co-owner, he'll inherit all the securities in that account at her death. Any siblings or other loved ones will be excluded, no matter what it says in your client's will.

Therefore, joint ownership reduces estate planning flexibility and may create gift tax problems. If clients are going to use joint ownership, they may want to restrict it to a checking account that holds a relatively small amount of money.

Execute a medical power of attorney, too.

There are other tools that should be used as part of an incapacity plan. Your clients should have not only a durable power of attorney,

> **Your clients should have not only a durable power of attorney, they should have a medical power of attorney, too.**

they should have a medical power of attorney, too. Such a document, which may be known as a health care power or a medical directive, enables a family member to make medical decisions if the patient can't.

A health care power of attorney might help prevent life-prolonging medical procedures when there's no chance of recovery. Your clients can name a different agent for a health care power of attorney than for a durable power of attorney. In a given family, the sibling who has the most medical knowledge might have this authority while the sibling with the most financial expertise might be named on the durable power of attorney.

Draw up a living will.

Living wills don't replace traditional wills but they state the circumstances in which someone will want doctors to withhold or withdraw life-support systems.

Key Document Preparation

In addition, some basic estate planning moves may be beneficial in incapacity planning.

- **Review key papers**. In the situation mentioned above, when 90-year-old Mike Harris began to deteriorate, his son Dan made certain that his father's financial documents were in order. The family wanted to make it easier to make lifetime gifts, for estate planning purposes, and to provide for an easy transition when the estate would go through probate.

- **Round up investment records**. As long as Mike Harris had most of his memory, family members could trace his cost basis in his securities, which will help his family resolve tax issues in the future.

  Middle-aged clients might advise their parents to consolidate securities into one investment account. Otherwise, elderly people may have stocks all over the place, with securities in their own name and at several brokerage firms. If all of these securities are rounded up and held at one brokerage firm, that will make it easier for the family to keep track. Then, if the elderly person wants dividends and interest to be paid into a bank account, that can be arranged.

- **Make sure documents are accessible**. Beyond securities, other paperwork should be accounted for. Some elderly people keep powers of attorney or trust documents in their safe deposit box. Then, if the elderly person becomes incapacitated, those papers won't be accessible when they're needed. Instead, these and other important documents should be kept where family members can get at them at any time.

Putting the Pieces Together: Developing an Incompetency Plan

Several of these elements may be combined to form an overall incompetency plan. For example, George Peters was a veterinarian who spent a great deal of his time buying and managing real estate. Now George is near 80, in a second marriage to a much younger woman, and "scared of Alzheimer's," as he puts it. He wants to provide for his daughter from his first marriage and keep his assets from winding up in the hands of his wife's two children.

Therefore, George has created this plan:

- His investments have been donated to a charitable remainder trust. Creating such a trust not only will generate a sizable tax deduction for a charitable contribution, it also can be structured to pay George a lifetime income. The trust fund eventually will go to his alma mater and the local symphony, his favorite causes. George has received recognition from both of these organizations, which is very important to him.

- Another trust has been created to buy and hold a large life insurance policy, payable to his wife; the premiums will be paid by tax savings and income from the charitable trust.

- A third trust is revocable. (The charitable remainder trust and the life insurance trust are irrevocable.) George has put his real estate holdings in there and named himself as trustee, so he can continue to manage the properties, which is what he really likes to do.

- George also has executed a durable power of attorney, naming his daughter as his agent.

Now, if George is stricken with Alzheimer's and can't manage his own affairs, the charitable trust will continue to pay out income. George's daughter can use the power of attorney to take over George's day-to-day finances such as paying bills. Control of the investment property, held in the revocable trust, will pass to the co-trustee, a local trust company. Thus, the properties will be maintained so they can eventually go to the daughter. The vet has income and recognition; caretakers are in place in case he becomes incompetent; and his wife and daughter will both be provided for at his death.

> With an incapacity plan in place your clients will have much more flexibility to adapt to changing circumstances.

Preparation Can Pay Off

Incapacity planning may be an important part of an LTC plan. Suppose, for example, Victoria Russell is a widow with $200,000 in assets. If she has a stroke or falls victim to Alzheimer's, she'll likely have to go into a nursing home. Those assets will have to be used to pay nursing home bills, as long as she resides there. In case of a long stay, all of those assets could be spent before her bills are paid by Medicaid.

Consider what might have happened with an incapacity plan. If her son William is named the agent under a durable power of attorney, he could make gifts and thus protect assets for himself and other family members.

Assume that the nursing home Victoria is in costs $6,000 per month and she has income of $3,000 a month from Social Security and a pension. Thus, the shortfall is $3,000 per month.

In this case, William might transfer $132,000 worth of his mother's assets to himself and his siblings, leaving their mother $68,000. The waiting period would be 22 months (the $132,000 transfer divided by the $6,000 monthly cost) but Victoria's $68,000 could be used to pay those bills.

After that time, William can apply for Medicaid on his mother's behalf because the waiting period will have expired: he'll have saved the family $132,000!

Naturally, you'll want to work with an experienced attorney on any such strategy. However, with an incapacity plan in place your clients will have much more flexibility to adapt to changing circumstances. Without such a plan, there may be little that can be done.

Reality Check

All of this planning may make sense on paper, but it's not always easy in the real world. How can your client, a middle-aged daughter, tell her father that he's losing his competency and ask for a power of attorney? One approach is to mention problems other elderly people are having managing their own affairs and then suggest some steps a parent can take in order to avoid the difficulties afflicting acquaintances.

Some elderly parents are extremely secretive, with a desire to remain in control. They're worried that they'll have enough to live on. Therefore, your clients may be better off bringing in a third-party, such as a financial planner, to assure parents that they'll have enough while explaining the need for taking certain measures. As a professional, you may be better at describing the situation and the recommendations may not sound as selfish as they would if they came from a middle-aged son or daughter.

Many elderly people don't even want to think about incapacity— they consider it a fate worse than death. Still, your clients should raise the issue with their parents, to see if the parents are open to a discussion. If they are, you can enter the picture as a third-party advisor who'll be seen as impartial. That way your clients and their parents can have a plan ready so that someone can step in quickly, if it becomes necessary.

Caring Community

There's yet another way to cope with concerns about incapacity and LTC: move into a continuing care community. Such communities can offer a continuum, from independent living through custodial care. Often, they provide a range of activities that may make retirement more enjoyable — but at a cost.

How should you suggest clients proceed, if they want to find a suitable community?

- **Look around before leaping**. Patience and prudence pay off. Clients should take a look at more than one community in the region they've chosen. In many communities they can take a short-term rental to see what living there will be like.

- **Read the fine print**. Get a copy of the contract and go over it before clients sign. If you have any doubts, tell your clients to keep looking.

Some people buy into a retirement community and pay $50,000 or more for a full membership in the country club, only to discover that they don't like the facilities or the other members. Your clients are better off renting in the community for a year or two, perhaps taking a "social" membership in the club at a much lower price. Whenever clients are making a major change in living arrangements it pays to browse before buying.

Site Visits Important

There are retirement living communities that offer a range of independent living, assisted living, and custodial care. Generally, people move into these communities while they're still healthy, able to enjoy the swimming pools, golf courses, and other facilities. If they decline in vigor, they move to different levels within the community.

Again, site visits may be especially important — tell clients not to be sold by a spectacular brochure. Instead, they should stay at least one night in a guest house or guest room before making any decisions. Suggest they eat some meals in the communal dining room to make sure they like the food and the atmosphere.

Low-Pressure Appeal

You can judge a retirement community by the way it sells itself.

- **Shy away from salespeople**. Reputable communities won't pressure prospects to sign up. Instead, they'll ask a lot of questions, trying to determine whether a prospect will be happy there.

  You should be especially skeptical about a community that has been around for several years and has an occupancy rate under 85%. Good retirement communities fill up rapidly.

- **Money matters**. Some continuing care communities demand up-front fees of $50,000, $100,000, and up. Such fees may be partially or fully non-refundable. (Often, the money from a house sale provides the cash necessary to enter a continuing care community.)

  If your clients are going to invest that much in a retirement community, you should ascertain that the investment is sound. A retirement community must have statements showing assets, liabilities, and net income; these statements should be audited by a reputable professional.

  If a community won't show you its current financial statements, tell your clients to walk away. You'll want some assurance the community won't go bankrupt after your clients have moved in.

A Healthy Home

Check out a community's medical facilities, too.

- **Nursing service**. Some communities have a registered nurse on-premises 24-hours-a-day, every day. In other communities, the nurse's hours may be limited to 9-5 on weekdays. Find out what nursing services are available, and, if there are gaps, what fallbacks the community provides.

- **Hospital affiliation**. Similarly, you should find out if a community has arrangements with a nearby hospital or clinic for medical situations that require a physician rather than a registered nurse. A relationship with a renowned medical center may be extremely reassuring.

- **Custodial care.** One of the main reasons for paying a sizable upfront fee for admission to a continuing care community is to gain access to nursing home care. Nevertheless, all long-term care isn't equal; so you should inspect those facilities carefully.

Find out if there are enough nursing beds to serve all those who need care. If you're representing a married couple, ask what extra costs will be involved if one spouse needs nursing care while the other remains in their former residence.

Chapter 8

CONCLUSION

Why Consider Long-Term Care Now?

Most people, including myself, look forward to leading a long and healthy life. This positive outlook, some feel, is at odds with the whole concept of long-term care. Some would even argue that preparing for long-term care needs is a negative approach that becomes a self-fulfilling prophecy by presupposing the need for long-term assistance. I strongly disagree. For several reasons, it is actually prudent, practical, and ultimately, a very positive and healthy exercise to prepare for long-term needs as early in life as possible.

First, our parents, clients, loved ones — as well as each and every one of us — will get older one day, and our health and ability to care for ourselves or a loved one will diminish over time. Meeting the issues, head-on, NOW, means not being forced by circumstances to make important decisions while under the "emotional gun," down the road.

The issue of skyrocketing medical costs is another critical factor. We're all conscious of how inflated health-care costs could rob us, in our old age, of dignity and independence. The same holds true for a catastrophic accident or illness in the prime of our lives. If costs continue to be prohibitive — and prior provisions have not been made to accommodate them — the medical-care alternatives for you, your clients and their families will be very limited and even undesirable.

What This Book Has Given You

Not everyone needs long-term care insurance, as this book has pointed out. But all of us—young or old, single, married or involved with someone—should take the time to make rational decisions about our long-term care needs. With proper planning, future care, and that of our clients, will not be a burden to our families.

This book was not meant to be the most comprehensive source of information available to you on the subject. The goal was merely to provide you with enough information to sort through the many factors, and make logical choices, appropriate to your particular circumstance. These choices will allow you and others to live out your golden years with respect, dignity, and the peace of mind that comes from knowing you have not become a burden, or unnecessarily depleted the family estate.

Another objective of this book has been to provide you with a resource for obtaining more information on given topics, more help evaluating particular scenarios, and additional means for ensuring that you, or your clients, are receiving all benefits purchased.

Overall, this book should have provided you with background and support material on the most common issues related to long-term care decisions, including:

- The best ways to fund long-term care, and options if financial resources are not available.

- The criteria needed to qualify for government-care programs, such as Medicaid and for determining if that's the best solution for you.

- Evaluating long-term care settings and facilities. What are the choices? How do you guarantee that choices are honored?

- All about what long-term care insurance policies do and do not cover: Are they affordable? What benefits are right for each situation?

Start thinking about these issues now. I truly hope no reader will need long-term care. But realistically—as a son, a father, a spouse, and an advisor—I know someone in my realm will need to handle these decisions at some point. They can be emotionally gut-wrenching when made under duress, during an emotionally distressing time.

If you think them through now, though, these difficult choices will be made infinitely easier for all involved. And, they'll be structured to preserve income, savings, dignity, independence, and—most importantly—peace of mind.

Here are a handful of questions you can start pondering, now, which are likely to come up down the road:

- **Facilities:** Will I/my parents be comfortable in a Medicaid facility if it is necessary?

- **Costs:** Can I afford a long-term care policy for me/my parents? Will it cost us more if we wait? Can we obtain the same benefits if we wait?

- **Care Giving:** Will I be able to function as a caregiver? Will I be able to get necessary time off from work or away from my own family that's required to be a caregiver?

- **Family Support:** What assistance can be reasonably expected from family members and others?

- **Second Spouse Situations:** Will we need to consider the wishes of a second spouse? Will we want to be responsible for the second spouse? How will we share responsibilities with the relatives of the second spouse.

I urge you to discuss these and other matters, now, with loved ones or clients. A frank and open dialogue is sure to help you reach conclusions that best suit you, your clients, or your family—for the long term.

Chapter 9

SUGGESTED RESOURCES

Favorite Sites

- **www.insuranceplanningadvisors.com**
  Halloran Financial Services, specialists in estate and financial planning, providing comprehensive solutions for insurance and long-term care needs for over 20 years. For information contact:
  Halloran Financial Services
  Mike@insuranceplanningadvisors.com
  781-449-4556
  400 Hillside Ave, Needham, MA 02494

- **www.ltcshelton.com**
  Phyllis Shelton of LTC Consultants, Nashville, Tennessee, offers LTC sales training to financial planners on her Web site.

- **www.weissratings.com/LTC_plan_intro.asp**
  For a free LTC insurance planning guide go on-line or send a self-addressed, stamped, business-size envelope to LTC Planner, Weiss Ratings, 4176 Burns Road, Palm Beach Gardens, FL 33410.

- For a list of LTC insurance policies and description of features:
  www.ltcibuyersadvocate.com (Long Term Care Insurance Buyers Advocate) and **www.aarp.org/confacts/health/privltc.html** (AARP).

- For price quotes on LTC insurance:
  www.gefn.com/longtermcare/afford_insurance/cost/estimator.html and **www.tiaa-cref.org/ltc/ltc_quote.html**

- **www.hiaa.org/consumer/ltcdirec.cfm** (The Health Insurance Association of America) lists member insurers that sell LTC policies.

- **www.aahsa.org** (The American Association of Homes and Services for the Aging) has information on what separates an average nursing home from an excellent one.

- For leads in the area of lifetime settlements, visit or call: **www.nationalviatical.org** (National Viatical Association, 800-741-9465) or **www.hivpositive.com** (Viatical Association of America, 202-429-5129).

Hot Lines

Here are key phone numbers for tracking down resources to assist you in planning for your aging clients:

Eldercare Locator Service **800-677-1116**
A national directory of community services.

Alzheimer's Association **800-272-3900**
Will recommend local support groups.

National Academy of Elder Law Attorneys **520-881-4005**
Can refer you to a specialist practicing near your parents' home.

National Association of Professional
Geriatric Care Managers **520-881-8008**
The clearinghouse for entrepreneurs who'll put together a package of aides, nurses, companions, etc.

Check your local Yellow Pages under Home Health Services to find people who'll care for your parents in their home.

Suggested Reading List

Planning For Long-Term Care
by United Seniors Health Council

This book demystifies the issues surrounding long-term care insurance so readers can make informed decisions when buying a policy. You'll learn how to access long-term care services as well as how to pay for them. It's a must-have guide for anyone that's looking into long-term care for themselves or a loved one.

$14.95   *Item #T136X-59024*

Long-Term Care: Your Financial Planning Guide
by Phyllis R. Shelton

Learn everything you need to know about long-term financial planning with this great guide. A comprehensive look that will help anyone who needs to plan for the future.

$16.00   *Item #T136X-17372*

Long-Term Care, 3rd Edition
by Jason Goetze

This fast-growing insurance market is also a key aspect of your clients' assets. Now, get training on the best solutions for the long-term care needs of your clients—while also picking up continuing education credit. Covers: Providers of long-term care, alternatives to it, a sample policy, underwriting guidelines, and much more!

$29.00   *Item #T136X-10171*

The Complete Idiot's Guide® to Long-Term Care Planning
by Marilee Driscoll

- Quick and easy ways to learn why the information exists
- Idiot-proof steps to understanding how the information affects you
- Comprehensive coverage of the consequences of the information

$19.95   *Item #T136X-604625*

J.K. Lasser's Choosing the Right Long-Term Care Insurance
by Benjamin Lipson

- Do's and don'ts of buying a policy
- What to expect when applying
- How to choose the best plan for you
- Keep your independence
- Advice for seniors and their children

$16.95   *Item #T136X-84383*

Long-Term Care Insurance Made Simple
by Les Abromovitz

- Maintain control over your medical care and protect your assets
- Determine if you need a long-term care policy and what kind
- Locate insurance, legal, financial, and medical, resources so you and your loved one can get the best care available

$14.95   *Item #T136X-565266*

Chapter 10

REVIEW YOUR KNOWLEDGE

There are numerous issues to consider when determining which long-term care options are appropriate for the various situations presented by your clients. And there are many variables to weigh and evaluate in order to make the best recommendations. I have tried to present a clear and up-to-date overview of the long-term care scenario that will not only make you more knowledgeable, but will also make you more comfortable with long-term care planning.

To help reinforce the information presented and to ensure you have absorbed the nuances and key points of each chapter, I am providing a chapter-by-chapter review quiz. It is crucial to your learning process that you take the time to read and to reflect upon the explanations given below just as you would any other portion of this book.

From Chapter I

Q. **Which government program is most likely to pay for the costs of long-term care?**
   A. Medicare
   B. Medicaid
   C. Medigap
   D. Social Security

A. (B) Medicaid, a federal-state poverty program, pays nearly half of all nursing home costs. In order to qualify, clients must first be impoverished. Although clients may think that Medicare will pay for long-term care, Medicare pays only for limited amounts of medically necessary care.

From Chapter II

Q. **In an assisted-living facility, staff members have more medical responsibilities than staff members in a nursing home.**
   A. True
   B. False

A. (B) False. People on staff at assisted-living facilities aren't allowed to give medication to residents (except for insulin shots.) They can remind residents about medication, but they can't put a pill into someone's mouth.

In nursing homes, an important staff function is administering medication, via pills, injections, or IV.

From Chapter III

Q. **Compared with regular Medicare and a Medigap supplement policy, a Medicare HMO is probably:**
   A. More expensive and more restrictive
   B. More expensive and less restrictive
   C. Less expensive and more restrictive
   D. Less expensive and less restrictive

A. (C) In a Medicare HMO, participants' out-of-pocket costs are reduced. In return, enrollees must use certain physicians, who are in the network. Often, they can't see a specialist without the permission of a generalist "gatekeeper."

Q. **Which Medicare supplement ("Medigap") insurance policies provide skilled nursing care?**
   A. A through J
   B. C through J
   C. F, G, I, J
   D. D, G, I, J

A. (B) Except for low-cost policies A and B, all Medigap policies cover the daily co-payments ($99 per day in 2001) for days 21 through 100 in a skilled nursing facility.

From Chapter IV

Q. Medicaid applicants must reveal all asset transfers made within the previous:

    A. 6 months

    B. 12 months

    C. 24 months

    D. 36 months

A. (D) Gifts and below-market sales within the previous 36 months must be reported. For transfers to trusts, the look-back period is 60 months.

Q. Joan Roberts lives in an area where the average nursing home costs $5,000 per month. She gives away $40,000 to her daughter Kathy, bringing Joan below the poverty line, as defined by Medicaid. Joan can apply to have Medicaid pay her nursing home bills after:

    A. 8 months

    B. 12 months

    C. 36 months

    D. 60 months

A. (A) Applicants must wait for a given number of months to apply. That number is the amount of assets transferred, divided by the average cost of local nursing homes. Here, $40,000 divided by $5,000 per month equals eight months.

From Chapter V

Q. In order to qualify for tax benefits, LTC policies must pay off if policyholders are unable to perform at least some activities of daily living (ADLs). How many ADLs must the policyholder be unable to perform?

    A. One

    B. Two

    C. Three

    D. Four

A. (B) Policyholders must be unable to perform at least two of these ADLs: eating, bathing, dressing, getting out of bed, using the toilet, and continence.

Q. You should advise clients to avoid LTC insurance policies from companies that practice back-end underwriting.

    A. True

    B. False

A. (A) True. Such companies accept virtually all applicants, regardless of their health. However, if a policyholder goes into a nursing home and files a claim for benefits, these insurers will try to find a pre-existing medical problem that wasn't revealed, in order to deny the claim. LTC policies from companies that do their underwriting upfront are harder to obtain but more likely to pay off.

From Chapter VI

Q. In order for the proceeds from a viatical settlement to be tax-free, a physician must certify that death is reasonably expected within:

    A. 6 months

    B. 12 months

    C. 24 months

    D. 36 months

A. (C) 24 months. In addition, the tax exemption will be available only if the payment comes from a "viatical settlement provider" who'll report the transaction to the IRS on Form 1099-LTC.

Q. A power of attorney that will remain in force even if the creator becomes incompetent is called a:

    A. Durable power of attorney

    B. Superior power of attorney

    C. Medical power of attorney

    D. Fiduciary power of attorney

A. (A) A durable power of attorney will remain in force, whether or not the creator is incompetent. A "springing" power of attorney will take effect only if the creator is unable to act on his or her own behalf.

Free 2-Week Trial Offer
for U.S. Residents from
Investor's Business Daily:

INVESTOR'S BUSINESS DAILY will provide you with the facts, figures, and objective news analysis you need to succeed.

Investor's Business Daily is formatted for a quick and concise read to help you make informed and profitable business and investment decisions.